When Thoughts Run Wild: A Mom's Guide to Untangling Cognitive Distortions

Ellie Hartfield

Published by Ellie Hartfield, 2024.

WHEN THOUGHTS RUN WILD: A MOM'S GUIDE TO UNTANGLING COGNITIVE DISTORTIONS

First edition. September 17, 2024.

Copyright © 2024 Ellie Hartfield.

ISBN: 979-8227905741

Written by Ellie Hartfield.

Table of Contents

When Thoughts Run Wild

A Mom's Guide to Untangling Cognitive Distortions

Introduction

————

Cognitive distortions are like those friends who mean well but always give you the wrong advice. They pop up uninvited, offering their misguided wisdom, urging you to see life in extremes, assume the worst, and place blame where it doesn't belong. If left unchecked, they can turn the simplest situations into a web of frustration and anxiety. When you're a mom balancing the chaos of two energetic kids, a freelancing career, a tech-enthusiast husband, and a sock-stealing dog named Max, these distortions have a way of sneaking into daily life, often catching you off guard.

Take "Polarized Thinking," for example, which suggests that you're either a perfect mom who has it all together or a complete disaster one Lego mishap away from ruin. Then there's "Mental Filtering," where your brain insists on highlighting the one minor parenting mistake you made that day while conveniently ignoring all the positives. It's as if these distortions come with a built-in magnifying glass, focusing only on the faults, the worries, and the what-ifs. But life, as we learn, is never black and white; it's a blend of messy colors, full of surprises that distortions rarely account for.

"Overgeneralization" loves to crash the party whenever something doesn't go as planned, whispering in your ear that this one event is proof that everything is destined to fail. And who could forget "Jumping to Conclusions," the distortion that gives you unsolicited mind-reading and fortune-telling skills? Suddenly, your son's quiet mood means he's definitely plotting a rebellion against bedtime, and that small hiccup in a family outing clearly predicts a full-scale disaster by noon. If only our thoughts had a mute button.

We then have "Catastrophizing" and "Personalization," those overzealous bodyguards of the mind. They rush in to blow small problems out of proportion and insist that you must be responsible for every single thing that goes wrong, from the weather to the sock shortage caused by Max. It's a relentless battle of keeping perspective amidst the whirlwind of responsibilities.

Somewhere between spilled milk and missed deadlines, the distortions can make you feel like you're constantly on trial, defending your worth as a parent, partner, and professional.

"Blaming" and "Labeling" work hand in hand to oversimplify complex situations. They direct your frustrations outward or inward with sweeping labels that do nothing but fuel resentment and self-doubt. The reality, however, is more nuanced. Kids misbehave, not because they've decided you're a bad parent, but because they're kids learning to navigate their emotions. Your husband's quirks aren't a personal affront; they're simply part of the tapestry that makes your family unique. The trick is learning to see beyond the labels and blames, recognizing the multifaceted nature of everyday life.

"Should Statements" and the "Fallacy of Change" trap you in a loop of unrealistic expectations, convincing you that life would be perfect if only everyone followed the unwritten script you have in your head. The truth is, life has its own script, full of plot twists, improvisations, and scenes that don't always make sense. "Emotional Reasoning" and "Control Fallacies" only add to the mix, turning fleeting feelings into perceived truths and suggesting you either have no control or are responsible for everything. It's a delicate dance, learning to accept that some things are within your power while others are not.

Finally, we face the "Fallacy of Fairness" and the "Heaven's Reward Fallacy," the persistent notions that life should play by a fair set of rules and that every sacrifice must lead to a reward. As much as we wish these rules applied, life often has other plans. Sometimes, the reward lies not in the outcome but in the effort itself. It's about finding joy in the process, laughing at the absurdities, and understanding that while cognitive distortions may never fully disappear, they can be managed with a mix of self-awareness, humor, and a little help from family.

Chapter 1 Polarized Thinking

———

1.1 Introduction to Polarized Thinking

Polarized thinking, also known as all-or-nothing thinking, is the mental trick that transforms life's colorful spectrum into a stark black-and-white film. It forces us to view situations in extremes—either you're a culinary genius whipping up five-star meals every night, or you're the parent who lets the kids eat cereal for dinner again (and again). There's rarely room for the middle ground, where reality actually lives. This type of thinking can be exhausting, turning daily challenges into emotional cliffhangers, where one slip-up feels like free-falling into an abyss of failure.

The effect of polarized thinking on daily life can be profound. It simplifies the complex, creating a false narrative that we must be one thing or the other, with no room for the muddled, beautiful mess in between. It's the voice that says if you didn't nail that presentation at work, you should probably consider a career change. Or if you didn't make it to yoga class this week, well, you're basically a couch potato now. The reality is far more nuanced, but polarized thinking thrives on the drama of extremes.

Definition and Psychological Basis of Polarized Thinking

POLARIZED THINKING is a defense mechanism that our brains use to help us make sense of the world. By categorizing experiences into neat boxes of "good" or "bad," it gives us a false sense of control. The world is a chaotic place, and our minds are constantly seeking ways to simplify the chaos into manageable chunks. When faced with uncertainty, our brains often jump to extremes as a way of avoiding the discomfort of ambiguity. It's as if the mind is saying, "If I can just label this situation as either completely wonderful or utterly terrible, then I can feel a little safer."

This mental pattern often develops as a way to shield us from potential harm. It's the same part of our brain that, back in the day, helped us decide quickly whether a rustle in the bushes meant a dangerous predator or just the wind. However, in our modern lives, this instinct can backfire. Instead of helping us dodge danger, it traps us in a cycle of high-stakes thinking. We end up believing that anything short of perfection is failure, and anything less than a disaster isn't worth worrying about.

The problem with polarized thinking is that it oversimplifies the complexity of our lives. It demands we make an immediate judgment—this is either good or bad, success or failure—without considering the myriad factors that make up our experiences. It's like watching only the first and last scenes of a movie and declaring you understand the whole plot. The rich, nuanced reality of life exists somewhere in the middle, but polarized thinking convinces us that the middle doesn't exist.

How Polarized Thinking Impacts Daily Decisions

THIS TYPE OF THINKING creeps into everyday decisions in subtle but pervasive ways. Take parenting, for example. It was last Halloween when my daughter decided she wanted to be a dragon—on the morning of October 31st. With no dragon costume in sight, I found myself frantically cutting up an old red sheet and stapling pieces of cardboard to form makeshift wings. My mind went into overdrive: "Either I create the perfect dragon costume in the next hour, or I'm the worst mom ever." Spoiler: the costume was a disaster, but my daughter loved it. And yet, there I was, convincing myself that because I hadn't made her look like she walked off a movie set, I had failed her in some grand way.

Then there's work. As a freelance graphic designer, deadlines are my life. One time, I had two projects overlap—a logo design for a local bakery and an ad campaign for an art festival. I managed to complete both, but in the logo design, I used a shade of blue that wasn't quite the right hue the client had envisioned. My brain jumped to, "If I can't even get the color right, I shouldn't be doing this at all." Never mind that the client was still thrilled with the final product. My mind latched onto that one small imperfection and labeled the entire project—and by extension, my career—as a failure.

Relationships aren't safe from this distortion either. Picture this: my husband leaves the dishes in the sink for the third night in a row. Polarized thinking swoops in with, "He's either the most thoughtful person or the messiest roommate ever. There's no in-between." In reality, he's just a busy guy who forgets sometimes, just like I do. But when we allow polarized thinking to dictate our perceptions, we miss the fact that most situations—and people—are a blend of strengths, flaws, and everyday forgetfulness.

The trouble is, polarized thinking feels convincing. It simplifies the world into digestible chunks that our brains can easily file away. But in doing so, it strips away the nuance, leaving us feeling like we're constantly on the edge of triumph or disaster. And when you live life at the extremes, it's hard to appreciate the small, beautiful moments that actually define our days.

Real-Life Example: Mom's All-or-Nothing Approach to Balancing Freelance Work and Parenting

I REMEMBER A PARTICULARLY chaotic week when polarized thinking took the wheel and drove me right into a stress-induced meltdown. It was the week of my son's preschool art show, and I had a major deadline for a graphic design project—a magazine cover for a local arts publication. My son had been working on a papier-mâché volcano for weeks, and he was beyond excited to show it off. Meanwhile, my client was eagerly awaiting a design that would capture the "vibrant artistic spirit" of our community. No pressure.

The night before the art show, I found myself in a precarious balancing act. There I was, hunched over my computer tweaking the magazine layout, while simultaneously trying to glue together pieces of cardboard for my son's volcano display board. Max, our ever-curious dog, decided it was the perfect moment to steal the glue stick, running through the house like a mischievous thief. My brain went into overdrive: "You're either a devoted mom or a professional designer—you can't be both."

The next day was a whirlwind. I delivered the magazine cover just hours before the art show and rushed to the school, only to find out I had forgotten to bring the extra baking soda for the volcano's eruption. My son gave me a look—half understanding, half disappointment. My brain, always eager to jump to extremes, whispered, "You failed both." The client was happy with the magazine, my son's volcano erupted beautifully (thanks to a quick rescue by his teacher), but all I could think about was how I didn't have it all perfectly together.

It was only later, as I recounted the story to my husband over dinner, that I realized how ridiculous it all sounded. "So let me get this straight," he said, barely containing his laughter. "You managed to finish a major project, attend an art show, and pull off a volcanic eruption, but because Max stole the glue stick and you forgot the extra baking soda, the whole day was a failure?" When he put it that way, it was clear how polarized my thinking had been.

In reality, that day was a success in its own messy, imperfect way. My son was proud of his volcano, my client loved the magazine cover, and yes, Max had a field day with the glue stick. But in my polarized thinking, I had been convinced that not doing everything flawlessly meant I had failed across the board. It was a perfect example of how this kind of thinking blinds us to the middle ground, where life actually happens.

1.2 Overcoming Polarized Thinking

THE FIRST STEP IN OVERCOMING polarized thinking is to catch yourself in the act. Recognize when your brain is throwing you into an all-or-nothing scenario. When you hear that little voice saying, "If I don't do this perfectly, it's a total failure," take a moment to pause and challenge that thought. Ask yourself, "Is there really no middle ground here? What's the most realistic way to view this situation?" Often, you'll find that the truth is somewhere in between.

Another strategy is to practice looking for the "gray areas" in your experiences. Life is not a series of win-or-lose moments; it's full of shades of gray. When things don't go as planned, remind yourself that it doesn't mean everything was a disaster. It just means that life happened, and you did your best with what you had. Accepting that most situations are a mix of successes and challenges can help you approach life with more compassion for yourself and others.

It's also crucial to embrace imperfection. We live in a world that often praises perfection, but perfection is an illusion. By allowing yourself to be human—to make mistakes, to be messy, and to not have it all figured out—you open the door to a more balanced mindset. When you let go of the need to always get it right, you free yourself to enjoy the moments that are, more often than not, wonderfully imperfect.

Thinking in Shades of Gray

TO BREAK FREE FROM polarized thinking, practice seeing life in shades of gray. When you catch yourself in an all-or-nothing mindset, ask, "What's the middle ground here?" For instance, after delivering a design project that didn't turn out exactly as I had envisioned, my immediate thought was, "This is a failure." But was it really? The client was satisfied, and I learned a few valuable lessons in the process. It wasn't a resounding triumph, nor was it a catastrophe. It was simply a project that had its strengths and areas for improvement.

Life rarely operates on a binary scale. Think about the time I attempted to cook a new Mediterranean dish for dinner. It was a bit of a culinary experiment involving saffron rice and a blend of spices I could barely pronounce. The result was... mixed. The rice was slightly undercooked, and the flavor wasn't quite what I'd hoped for. My initial thought was, "Well, that was a disaster." But then I noticed my husband and kids enjoying the meal, even though it was far from perfect. It wasn't a masterpiece, but it wasn't a failure either—it was an adventure.

Learning to think in shades of gray helps us appreciate life for what it is: a series of moments that are neither purely good nor purely bad. It's about recognizing that success and failure often coexist, and that's perfectly okay. By embracing the middle ground, we start to see our experiences in a more balanced light. Sometimes, life is just a mix of cooked and undercooked rice, and that's more than enough.

Learning to Accept Imperfections

PERFECTION IS AN ILLUSION, and accepting imperfections is a crucial step in overcoming polarized thinking. Let's take relationships as an example. For the longest time, I believed that a perfect family meant a spotless house, perfectly behaved children, and a perpetually cheerful atmosphere. But then reality set in. Kids spill things, arguments happen, and some days, the house looks like a tornado just swept through. Does this mean our family is failing? Absolutely not.

Accepting imperfections means embracing the messiness of life. In my graphic design work, I've learned that not every project will turn out exactly as I imagined. There have been times when the final design didn't match the vision I had in my head. But in many cases, it ended up being better in ways I hadn't expected. Letting go of the need for perfection opens the door for creativity, spontaneity, and the occasional pleasant surprise.

In parenting, embracing imperfection means recognizing that there will be days when screen time exceeds the recommended limit, or when dinner is a last-minute pizza delivery. It's about understanding that these moments don't define you as a parent. They are simply part of the ever-evolving journey of raising children. By accepting that imperfection is not only inevitable but also a natural part of life, you free yourself from the constant pressure of trying to live up to impossible standards.

When you accept that flaws and mistakes are part of the human experience, you become more compassionate toward yourself and others. Relationships flourish when there's room for imperfection. Projects become more enjoyable when you stop striving for a flawless outcome. And most importantly, life becomes richer when you allow yourself to be perfectly imperfect.

Conversation with Husband: All-or-Nothing Attitudes in Family Life

ONE EVENING, AFTER the kids had gone to bed and the house was finally quiet, I brought up my all-or-nothing mindset to my husband. "I feel like I'm either killing it as a mom or failing miserably," I confessed as we sat down with a glass of wine. He looked at me with a mix of empathy and amusement. "So, are we talking about the same day you managed to do laundry, cook dinner, and still have time to help our son with his school project?" he asked, a grin forming on his face.

"Yes," I said, a little defensively. "But dinner was just spaghetti, and the laundry is still in the dryer." He chuckled. "Okay, but did anyone starve? And did our son seem upset about the 'just spaghetti' dinner?" I thought back to our son slurping up noodles and giggling at the strands hanging from his mouth. "No," I admitted. "He loved it."

He leaned back and took a sip of his wine. "You see, this is what I mean. You're looking at everything like it has to be perfect or it's a disaster. But most of the time, things just are. And that's not a bad thing." I knew he was right. My tendency to view life through an all-or-nothing lens often overshadowed the fact that our family life was full of little wins, even if they didn't fit into my idea of 'perfect.'

We started joking about the other times I had fallen into this mindset. Like the day I forgot to pack my daughter's dance shoes and spent the entire class convincing myself I was the worst mom on the planet. "She danced in socks and had a blast," my husband reminded me. "You turned it into a disaster in your head, but for her, it was just another fun class." He had a point. To my daughter, it was a memorable moment. To me, it was another tally in the 'fail' column.

By the end of our conversation, we had agreed to start calling each other out on our all-or-nothing thinking. Whether it was him feeling like he was failing at work because of one missed deadline or me thinking our house had to be Instagram-ready at all times, we decided to remind each other that life happens in the messy middle. It was a small but significant step toward embracing a more balanced, realistic view of our lives.

Chapter 2 Mental Filtering

2.1 Negative Mental Filtering

Negative mental filtering is like having a mental sieve that catches only the unpleasant bits of life, while all the good stuff slips right through. It's when your brain decides to spotlight the one thing that went wrong, ignoring everything else that went right. You might have hosted a delightful dinner party, full of laughter and delicious food, but what you remember is the one dish that came out a bit overcooked. This focus on the negative turns what should be a balanced view into a skewed, distorted reality.

Living with this filter can make daily life feel like a series of minor disasters. It becomes a habit of replaying that one awkward comment you made at the book club meeting, forgetting that everyone else was probably too busy enjoying the wine and conversation to notice. The more the negative filter takes over, the harder it becomes to see the whole picture. Positive moments start to fade into the background, while the negatives take center stage, leaving you with a sense of inadequacy that doesn't match the reality of your experiences.

This mental pattern doesn't just affect how you view individual events; it colors your entire outlook on life. A lovely day at the beach becomes overshadowed by the one moment when your ice cream fell off the cone. A successful work project is tainted by the one minor typo in the final report. It's a mental habit that makes the world seem harsher and more unforgiving than it truly is, stealing joy from moments that deserve to be cherished.

Explanation and Psychological Basis of Mental Filtering

MENTAL FILTERING IS a cognitive bias that has roots in our brain's survival mechanisms. From an evolutionary standpoint, focusing on negative events helped our ancestors survive. If you're walking through the jungle, it's more crucial to notice the snake in the grass than to admire the beautiful flowers around you. Our brains evolved to prioritize potential threats over positive stimuli, ensuring that we remained alert to dangers in our environment. This negativity bias was once a lifesaver but in the modern world, it often causes unnecessary stress.

This bias has a lot to do with how our brain processes information. When an event occurs, the brain tends to latch onto anything that seems like a threat or a failure. It then magnifies that detail, replaying it over and over to "learn" from it, even when there's not much to learn. While this process was useful when the "threat" was a wild animal, it's less helpful when the "threat" is an awkward conversation or a minor mistake in a work email. The brain doesn't distinguish between the two; it reacts to both with the same level of intensity.

Moreover, mental filtering often develops as a result of past experiences. If you've faced criticism or high expectations throughout your life, your brain may become conditioned to focus on what goes wrong, assuming that this is what needs to be fixed. It's a habit that, while formed with good intentions—self-improvement, awareness—ends up narrowing your focus to only the negatives, leaving the positives in the dark. The result is a skewed perception of reality, where the negatives seem more prominent than they actually are.

Personal Example: Fixating on Minor Parenting Mistakes

A CLASSIC EXAMPLE OF mental filtering in action happened one chaotic morning. My daughter had an important school event, and she insisted on wearing her favorite unicorn dress. I was multitasking, trying to get my son to finish his cereal, pack lunches, and make sure everyone had brushed their teeth. Amid the whirlwind, I managed to iron her unicorn dress—a feat that should have earned me some sort of parenting award. But then, disaster struck: I accidentally burned a tiny hole in the hem with the iron.

It was a small, barely noticeable hole, but to my brain, it might as well have been a gaping tear. My daughter didn't even seem to care; she was already twirling around the living room, dress fluttering, blissfully unaware. But I was stuck, fixating on that tiny imperfection. I replayed the moment in my head all morning: "How could I have been so careless? What kind of mother ruins her daughter's favorite dress right before a big event?" Never mind that we got out the door on time, with packed lunches and brushed hair—the day had already been labeled a failure in my mind.

That one minor mistake overshadowed the rest of the day. I sat through the school event, watching my daughter proudly show off her outfit, but all I could focus on was the tiny burn mark. It was ridiculous, really. No one else noticed. My husband later told me, "She looked adorable, and she had a blast. Why are you so hung up on it?" But my brain had latched onto the "error," filtering out everything else—the smiles, the laughter, the fact that she had a great time.

It wasn't until much later that I realized how my mental filter had stolen the joy of that day. Instead of seeing the whole picture—my daughter's happiness, the overall success of the morning—I had zeroed in on one insignificant flaw. The dress was just fine, and so was I. It was a lesson in how mental filtering can amplify minor missteps, turning them into defining moments when, in reality, they're just tiny blips in the grand scheme of things.

Playful Scene: Kids Teasing Mom About "The Great Pancake Fire"

OF COURSE, MY KIDS have a knack for bringing perspective back with their unique sense of humor. Take "The Great Pancake Fire" incident. One Sunday morning, in my grand attempt to make a perfect breakfast, I decided to try a new recipe—fluffy blueberry pancakes with lemon zest. I was feeling ambitious, maybe a little too ambitious. As I focused on getting the batter just right, I didn't notice that the pan was heating up to an inferno-level temperature. When I finally poured the batter, it was like an instant volcanic eruption. Smoke billowed, the fire alarm blared, and Max the dog sprinted for cover under the table.

The kids came running into the kitchen, eyes wide with excitement. "Are we having pancakes or is this an experiment?" my son asked, peeking around the doorway with a grin. I was mortified. "It's ruined," I muttered, waving a dish towel at the smoke alarm, which by now was screaming at a pitch only dogs and mortified mothers could hear. I mentally filed the morning under "Epic

Fail," certain that my dream of a cozy, picture-perfect breakfast was now just a charred memory.

But my kids? They thought it was the funniest thing ever. The next day at school, they proudly recounted "The Great Pancake Fire" to their friends, exaggerating the details in the way only kids can. "The kitchen was full of smoke, and Mom was like a firefighter!" my daughter told her class. To them, it wasn't a disaster; it was an adventure. In their eyes, the morning wasn't ruined—it was made memorable.

Their playful teasing continued for weeks. "Mom, do we need a fire extinguisher before you start dinner?" they'd joke whenever I reached for a frying pan. It became a family legend, a story we laughed about rather than cringed at. They helped me see that one small mishap didn't define our morning or my abilities as a mom. In fact, it became one of those shared memories that made our family feel closer. And, for what it's worth, the cereal we ended up having instead of pancakes was pretty great.

2.2 Disqualifying the Positive

DISQUALIFYING THE POSITIVE is a cousin of negative mental filtering, and it's just as sneaky. This cognitive distortion convinces you that even when you succeed, it doesn't really count. Did you complete that project on time? Well, it wasn't that hard, right? Got a compliment on your homemade lasagna? They're probably just being polite. It's the internal mechanism that brushes aside your wins, big or small, rendering them meaningless in the grand narrative of "not enough."

This mindset can be incredibly draining. It's like having a mental referee that constantly declares every victory null and void. You could be juggling a dozen responsibilities, meeting every challenge, and still find a way to convince yourself it wasn't "good enough." The problem is that this habitual dismissal of your accomplishments trains your brain to focus solely on shortcomings, further reinforcing a narrative of inadequacy.

The tragedy of disqualifying the positive is that it robs you of the joy that comes from acknowledging your efforts. You become blind to your own strengths and achievements, perpetually stuck in a cycle of striving without ever feeling like you've truly succeeded. It's a never-ending race where the finish line keeps moving just out of reach, leaving you exhausted and unable to appreciate how far you've come.

Husband's Encouragement to Acknowledge Success

ONE EVENING, AFTER finally finishing a complex design project for a new client's art exhibit, I found myself in my usual post-project slump. My husband asked how it went, and I launched into a list of everything that could have been better: the color palette wasn't as bold as I'd hoped, the typography wasn't as edgy. He listened patiently before interrupting me with, "But wasn't the client thrilled? Didn't they say it was exactly what they envisioned?"

I shrugged. "Yeah, but they probably just said that to be nice. It could have been so much better if I had just spent more time on the font selection." He sighed and shook his head. "You know, you're like the only person I know who can climb a mountain and then complain about the view at the top." I looked at him, confused. "What do you mean?"

He put down his book and looked at me seriously. "You did something impressive. You met a challenging deadline, you put in the effort, and the client is happy. Why can't you just let yourself feel good about that? Why does everything have to be perfect for it to count?" His words hung in the air like a much-needed reality check. For a moment, I realized how often I had disqualified my own hard work. It was a stark reminder that acknowledging success is not about settling for less but about giving yourself permission to appreciate your efforts.

Emotional Shift: Moving from Self-Doubt to Self-Acceptance

THAT CONVERSATION MARKED the beginning of an emotional shift for me. I started small, trying to catch myself in the act of disqualifying my successes. The next time I finished a project, I made a conscious effort to acknowledge what went well instead of diving straight into self-critique. It wasn't easy; old habits die hard. I remember the first time I deliberately paused to appreciate my work: I had designed a poster for a local theater production, and instead of nitpicking it to death, I allowed myself to step back and think, "That turned out pretty good."

It felt strange, almost uncomfortable, to give myself credit. My mind wanted to jump to every tiny detail that could have been different, but I resisted. As days went by, I noticed that this small practice started to change the narrative in my head. I began to see that success doesn't have to mean flawless execution. It can simply mean doing your best, learning from the experience, and feeling proud of what you've accomplished.

The real breakthrough came during an ordinary day when I managed to juggle work calls, school pick-up, and making dinner without falling into my usual pattern of self-criticism. I stood in the kitchen, stirring a pot of pasta, and thought, "Today was a win." It wasn't perfect—there were a few chaotic moments, a minor spill here and there—but it was enough. The kids were happy, the work got done, and dinner wasn't burnt. For once, I allowed myself to feel that sense of accomplishment without mentally tearing it down.

The shift from self-doubt to self-acceptance was gradual and imperfect, but it was transformative. I learned that accepting success doesn't mean you stop striving for growth. It means you recognize your own effort and give yourself the grace to be proud of what you've achieved. It's about embracing the fact that your best effort, in whatever form it comes, is worthy of acknowledgment.

Playful Footnote: Max Never Disqualifies His Positive Sock-Stealing Successes

IF THERE'S ANYONE WHO embodies the concept of celebrating success without hesitation, it's Max, our dog. He's the world champion of sock theft, and he's never shy about parading around with his "prizes." It doesn't matter if he only managed to snag a single, unmatched sock; he'll strut around the living room with the confidence of a gold medalist. He never pauses to think, "Well, I could have stolen two socks instead of one, so does this really count?"

Max's joyful attitude is a reminder that sometimes, we need to be a little more like him—unapologetically proud of our small wins. If he can celebrate a lone sock as if he's conquered the world, surely we can find it in ourselves to acknowledge our own successes, no matter how modest they may seem. Because in the end, it's not about the size of the achievement; it's about the joy of recognizing that you did something worth celebrating.

Chapter 3 Overgeneralization

3.1 Introduction to Overgeneralization

Overgeneralization is the habit of taking one negative experience and using it as "proof" that an entire aspect of life is doomed to fail. It's like hitting one wrong note during a piano recital and instantly believing you're the worst musician ever. This mindset amplifies isolated incidents into universal truths, casting a shadow over everything else. The brain latches onto one mistake and draws sweeping, often dramatic conclusions that ignore all evidence to the contrary.

When you live with this mindset, life becomes a series of exaggerated storylines where every stumble seems like a prelude to a tragic ending. Spill coffee on your shirt during a morning meeting? Clearly, the entire day is destined to go downhill. The brain creates a pattern where none exists, making small blunders feel like they are part of an inevitable cycle of failure.

Psychological Explanation of Overgeneralization

OUR BRAINS ARE NATURALLY wired to recognize patterns, a trait that has been essential for survival throughout human evolution. For early humans, noticing a pattern—like the rustle of leaves often signaling a predator's presence—was a matter of life and death. In today's world, this same tendency can lead us to create connections between unrelated events, particularly when they are negative. If we fail at something once, our brain might overgeneralize this failure to prevent us from facing a similar situation again, trying to protect us from potential harm.

When something goes wrong, the brain quickly generalizes the event as a way of bracing itself for future occurrences. It's like a mental shortcut that says, "I've seen this before, and it didn't end well." The problem is, this shortcut bypasses a more rational assessment of the situation, lumping unique events into a broad category of failure. This can lead to a persistent negative mindset, where each misstep feels like it's part of an inevitable downward trend.

Overgeneralization often escalates when emotions are involved. When we're feeling overwhelmed, anxious, or insecure, our brains are more likely to connect the dots in a negative way. A single mistake can trigger a cascade of thoughts that link together to form a bleak narrative about our abilities or future prospects. We begin to view ourselves and our lives through the lens of that one moment, rather than as a series of individual experiences.

Example: Overgeneralizing from a Creative Failure

A COUPLE OF MONTHS ago, I decided to host a "Cultural Arts and Crafts Night" for my kids and a few of their friends. The idea was to explore different cultures through various crafts. My grand vision was to create an elaborate, Japanese-inspired origami installation with the kids, complete with intricate cranes, frogs, and flowers. I spent the whole week researching origami techniques, convinced that this would be an unforgettable, enriching experience. It was going to be like a mini art festival right in our living room.

The evening arrived, and the kids gathered around, wide-eyed and excited. I started by demonstrating a simple origami crane, but as I fumbled with the delicate folds, I realized I had vastly overestimated my paper-folding skills. The crane looked more like a crumpled paper airplane than the elegant bird I had envisioned. I tried again, but each attempt got worse. Soon, the kids were growing restless, losing interest in the craft that was turning into a struggle. My frustration mounted, and before I knew it, the "Cultural Arts Night" had dissolved into a chaotic mess of wrinkled paper and distracted children who had moved on to building forts out of couch cushions.

As I cleaned up the remnants of my failed origami dream, my mind started connecting dots that weren't there. "I'm not cut out for this. I can't even teach a simple craft. If I can't pull off one art night, how can I ever foster creativity in my kids?" My brain wasn't just focusing on that evening's flop; it was generalizing the incident to my entire role as a parent. I found myself brooding over past creative endeavors that hadn't gone perfectly, as if they all pointed to the same conclusion: I was failing at nurturing creativity in my children.

The next day, when my husband asked how the evening went, I described it as a disaster. He raised an eyebrow and asked, "Didn't the kids have fun building forts?" That simple question jolted me. In my overgeneralizing haze, I had completely missed the point. Sure, my origami project didn't go as planned, but the kids had a blast in their own way. To them, the night was an adventure, not a failure. Yet, my brain had taken one aspect of the evening—my failed craft—and painted the whole night, and my parenting, with a broad brush of failure.

3.2 Breaking the Overgeneralization Pattern

BREAKING FREE FROM overgeneralization involves recognizing when your brain is making leaps from one event to a universal judgment. When you catch yourself thinking that one misstep defines a whole aspect of your life, pause and question it. Ask yourself, "Is this one experience truly representative of everything?" Often, you'll find that it's not. The goal is to see events as isolated incidents rather than chapters in a never-ending saga of failure.

A helpful technique is to practice mindfulness and stay grounded in the present moment. Instead of letting your mind wander off into a narrative about how one event is indicative of a larger pattern, focus on what is happening right now. Ground yourself by acknowledging the facts of the situation without adding a layer of judgment. For example, "The origami didn't go as planned, but the kids had fun in a different way."

Another key strategy is to remind yourself of past successes and the uniqueness of each experience. Just because one creative night didn't go as planned doesn't mean all future attempts will fail. Every event is a new opportunity with different variables. By shifting your focus to this reality, you can break the habit of letting one experience dictate your overall narrative.

Shifting from All-or-Nothing Thinking to Balanced Reflection

SHIFTING FROM OVERGENERALIZATION to balanced reflection means taking a step back and looking at situations through a more nuanced lens. After the origami debacle, I decided to give myself a mental "time-out" before jumping to conclusions. I asked myself to reflect on the entire event, not just the part that went wrong. Sure, my crane-folding skills were laughable, but was the evening a complete disaster? The answer was no.

The kids did explore creativity, just not in the way I had originally planned. They ended up using the failed origami pieces as props for their fort games, turning my paper scraps into pirate maps and treasure chests. They were creative, imaginative, and most importantly, happy. The event wasn't about perfect origami but about exploring and having fun. When I took a balanced look at the evening, I realized that what I had labeled a "failure" was, in fact, a success in a different form.

Balanced reflection also means being gentle with yourself. It involves acknowledging that every effort is a learning experience, not a referendum on your abilities. By seeing the bigger picture, you can give yourself the grace to have off days and imperfect outcomes. It helps you appreciate that creativity—and life, for that matter—is not a series of perfect executions but a series of attempts, experiments, and yes, even happy accidents.

Playful Footnote: If Max Can Be Forgiven for One Sock Theft, So Can We

MAX, OUR SOCK-LOVING dog, provides a perfect example of why overgeneralization is often misplaced. If we were to overgeneralize his behavior, we'd declare him the "Perpetual Sock Thief," doomed to a life of petty laundry crimes. And yet, every time he trots into the room with a lone sock dangling from his mouth, we don't label him as a hopeless case. We laugh, forgive him, and move on. In our family, he's not defined by his sock-stealing episodes; he's a quirky, lovable part of our everyday chaos.

So why do we forgive Max for his repeated sock offenses but not ourselves for a single misstep? Maybe it's because we understand that Max's sock theft is just one small part of who he is—a mischievous but well-loved member of the family. If we can extend that kind of grace to a dog with an inexplicable fondness for footwear, surely we can find a way to do the same for ourselves. After all, one misstep doesn't define us, just like one stolen sock doesn't define Max.

Chapter 4 Jumping to Conclusions

4.1 Mind Reading

Mind reading is the mental trick where you assume you know exactly what others are thinking, and it's usually not something flattering. It's the moment when a friend doesn't immediately reply to your text, and your mind instantly decides they're mad at you. Or when your partner looks slightly preoccupied, and you're convinced they're upset about something you said (or didn't say) three days ago. This habit leads to an avalanche of assumptions, all based on nothing more than fleeting expressions or silences, leaving you tangled in a web of imagined scenarios.

Living with this mindset can feel like you're on a constant emotional detective mission, always searching for hidden meanings behind people's actions. A simple "Hmm" during a conversation turns into a mental unraveling of every word you've ever spoken to that person. In reality, they might just be thinking about what to have for lunch. The brain, however, convinces you that you've stumbled upon some unspoken truth, usually one that paints you in a less-than-favorable light.

Psychological Explanation of Mind Reading

MIND READING STEMS from our brain's desire to predict and understand social dynamics. We're naturally wired to read social cues as a way of navigating relationships and ensuring social harmony. However, this useful skill can morph into a distortion when it becomes overly sensitive to perceived negativity. The brain tends to interpret ambiguous cues—like a silence or a furrowed brow—as negative because it prepares us for potential threats or social rejection, a trait that helped our ancestors survive in tight-knit communities.

When we engage in mind reading, we're relying on incomplete information to draw conclusions. Our brains fill in the gaps with our own fears and insecurities, creating a narrative that often has little to do with reality. For example, if we're feeling insecure about a recent conversation, we're more likely to assume the other person is harboring negative thoughts about us. This thought process is automatic and often unconscious, driven by the brain's tendency to err on the side of caution to protect us emotionally.

Mind reading is particularly insidious because it thrives on ambiguity. The less information we have, the more room our minds have to fabricate stories. Silence, a neutral expression, or even a lack of a smile can become a blank canvas on which we project our deepest fears. The problem is, we rarely check if these assumptions are true, leading to a cycle of anxiety and unnecessary stress.

Example: Mom Assumes Her Kids Are Angry When They're Just Quiet

ONE SATURDAY AFTERNOON, I decided to take a break from work and join my kids in the living room, where they were deeply engrossed in building their latest Lego city. They were unusually quiet, huddled together in intense concentration. As I sat down, a sense of unease crept in. Why were they so quiet? Had I done something to upset them? My mind immediately raced through a checklist of potential offenses: Did I snap at them earlier when they asked for snacks? Did they overhear my phone call where I mentioned being stressed?

As the silence stretched on, I grew more convinced that they were upset. I cleared my throat and hesitantly asked, "Is everything okay? You two seem... quiet." My daughter glanced up briefly, blinked, and then returned to her Lego skyscraper. My son didn't even look up from his meticulous construction of what appeared to be a Lego moat. In my mind, this was it—proof that I had somehow disappointed them. They were giving me the silent treatment, clearly plotting to build a Lego fortress where they'd banish me for my parental shortcomings.

After a few more minutes of torturous silence, I couldn't take it anymore. "Are you sure everything's alright?" I pressed, attempting to sound casual but failing miserably. My son finally looked up, his expression one of mild confusion.

"Yeah, we're just trying to figure out how to make a drawbridge that actually works," he said matter-of-factly before diving back into his project. My daughter added, without looking up, "Yeah, Mom. We're busy. This is serious engineering."

I stared at them, stunned. They weren't upset. They were just absorbed in their Lego world, fully occupied with their grand architectural plans. My mind had concocted an entire narrative about their silence, complete with imaginary grievances and emotional turmoil, when in reality, they were simply building a castle. The "proof" I had gathered was nothing more than the silence of two kids focused on the task at hand, not a commentary on my parenting. It was a humbling reminder of how easily the mind can jump to conclusions based on assumptions rather than facts.

Humorous Husband Intervention: "Telepathic Parenting Powers"

LATER THAT EVENING, as I recounted the story to my husband, he listened with a bemused expression. "So let me get this straight," he said, trying not to laugh. "You thought the kids were silently judging you because they were... playing with Legos?" I nodded, feeling slightly sheepish. "Well, they were so quiet, and you know how they usually are," I explained. He shook his head, grinning. "Ah, I see. Your telepathic parenting powers were activated."

"Telepathic parenting powers?" I echoed, raising an eyebrow. "Yes," he continued with mock seriousness, "the ability to read our children's thoughts, no matter how absurdly inaccurate those readings might be. It's a very rare gift, you know. Not everyone can look at two kids building a Lego castle and deduce a full-blown family drama." He leaned back in his chair, clearly enjoying himself.

I laughed, despite myself. "Okay, okay, I get it. Maybe I jumped to conclusions," I admitted. "Maybe?" he replied, feigning shock. "You practically wrote an entire soap opera in your head, complete with the tragic 'Mom doesn't understand us' storyline." He made a dramatic gesture, covering his face with his hand. "Meanwhile, in the real world, they were constructing a drawbridge."

It was a lighthearted reminder of how ridiculous mind reading can be. While I was busy interpreting their silence as a sign of distress, my husband—ever the voice of reason—saw it for what it was: two kids, lost in the world of their imagination, with no room for anything else, including Mom's overactive telepathy. Sometimes, we need someone to gently poke fun at our mental acrobatics to bring us back to reality. As much as I hate to admit it, his "telepathic parenting powers" jab was spot-on.

4.2 Fortune Telling

FORTUNE TELLING IS the habit of predicting the future with an uncanny certainty that things will go wrong. It's the mental leap from "I have a presentation tomorrow" to "I'm going to bomb it, and everyone will think I'm incompetent." This distortion convinces you that you have a crystal ball, but it only shows you the worst-case scenarios. You find yourself dreading events before they even happen, convinced that disaster is not only possible but inevitable.

This mindset often leads to unnecessary anxiety, as you're constantly preparing for outcomes that may never come to pass. It's like carrying an umbrella everywhere because you're certain it's going to rain, even when the sky is clear. By assuming the worst, you rob yourself of the opportunity to experience life as it unfolds, often missing out on joy and spontaneity.

Psychological Explanation of Fortune Telling

FORTUNE TELLING STEMS from our brain's need to anticipate and prepare for possible threats. It's an offshoot of our fight-or-flight response, where the brain attempts to foresee potential dangers and prepare us to face them. In situations where the outcome is uncertain, our minds sometimes default to the worst-case scenario as a way of bracing ourselves for impact. It's a survival tactic that, while useful in life-threatening situations, often backfires in everyday life.

The brain leans toward negative predictions because it's wired to detect and respond to potential threats. Predicting a positive outcome doesn't trigger the same level of vigilance, so the mind tends to focus on what could go wrong to keep us on high alert. Unfortunately, this habit can lead to chronic stress, as we're constantly bracing for imaginary disasters.

Fortune telling can create a self-fulfilling prophecy. By expecting a negative outcome, you might unconsciously act in ways that make it more likely. For example, if you go into a family outing convinced it will be a disaster, you might approach it with a tense or anxious attitude, which can affect the mood of everyone involved. The very disaster you feared becomes more likely, not because of fate, but because of the mindset you brought into the situation.

Example: Mom Predicts Family Outings Will End in Chaos

ONE WEEKEND, I DECIDED to take the family to a nearby botanical garden that was hosting a special art-in-nature exhibit. It seemed like a perfect outing—art, nature, and a chance for the kids to burn off some energy. But as the day approached, my mind began to forecast the day's events. "It's going to be a nightmare," I thought. "The kids will get bored, they'll start complaining, someone will touch something they're not supposed to, and we'll have to leave early in a scene straight out of a disaster movie."

The morning of the outing, I found myself snapping at everyone. "Are we sure this is a good idea?" I asked my husband. "The botanical garden is bound to be crowded. What if they knock over one of the art pieces?" My husband gave me a look that said, "Here we go again," but wisely kept quiet. In my head, I had already envisioned the day spiraling out of control: spilled drinks, temper tantrums, and a stern lecture from a garden curator about touching the artwork.

With my dire predictions in tow, we set off. But as we arrived at the garden, the kids' faces lit up with awe. They were fascinated by the sculptures seamlessly integrated into the landscape. My daughter was mesmerized by a giant mosaic peacock, while my son became deeply involved in a scavenger hunt to find hidden ceramic creatures. They were engaged, enthusiastic, and, most surprisingly, well-behaved. The scene I had imagined—the chaos, the complaints—never materialized.

As we walked through the garden, my husband nudged me and whispered, "So, when does the disaster you predicted start?" I laughed, slightly embarrassed. "Maybe I was wrong," I admitted. "Maybe?" he teased. "You had us running for the exits before we even left the house." The day turned out to be a peaceful, joyful experience, the complete opposite of what I had so confidently forecasted.

By the end of the outing, the kids were happily exhausted, and we had enjoyed a picnic on the garden lawn, complete with butterfly sightings and some much-needed relaxation. My fortune telling had almost robbed me of this experience. It was a reminder that predicting disaster doesn't protect us; it only makes us miss out on the beauty that can unfold when we let go of our imagined catastrophes.

Playful Footnote: The Only Fortune Teller Here is Max, Who Predicts Dinner Time by Staring at the Fridge

IF THERE'S ANYONE IN our household who practices fortune telling, it's Max. But his predictions are laser-focused and accurate—he can predict dinner time with the precision of a seasoned psychic. He positions himself in front of the fridge an hour before his meal, staring at it with unwavering conviction, as if his sheer willpower will make it open faster. Max never worries about whether his dinner will arrive; he knows it will, eventually.

Max's confidence in his dinner predictions is a lighthearted contrast to my own fortune telling. While I predict chaos and disaster, he forecasts food and fulfillment. Perhaps we could all learn a bit from Max: instead of expecting the worst, maybe we should channel our inner canine and anticipate the good things, like dinner, coming our way.

Chapter 5: Catastrophizing

5.1 Magnification

Magnification is like wearing a pair of mental binoculars that turn every minor hiccup into a looming catastrophe. It's the moment when a small problem, like misplacing your keys, suddenly spirals into a full-blown disaster scenario: "I'll be late to work, my boss will think I'm unreliable, and I'll probably lose my job!" The brain races ahead, painting a picture of doom from what is, in reality, just a minor inconvenience. This cognitive distortion amplifies everyday challenges, making them feel insurmountable.

When magnification takes over, small issues begin to feel like they're about to end the world as you know it. A burnt dinner is no longer just a burnt dinner; it's a sign that you're failing at managing the household. A forgotten appointment isn't just a slip-up; it's the start of a downward spiral into total disorganization. Magnification turns molehills into mountains, leaving you stressed and overwhelmed by the smallest of missteps.

Psychological Explanation of Magnification

MAGNIFICATION OCCURS because the brain is hardwired to focus on potential threats and dangers. This cognitive distortion is rooted in our evolutionary past, where being hyper-aware of potential problems increased our chances of survival. If early humans magnified the significance of a rustling bush, it might have meant the difference between evading a predator or becoming lunch. However, in modern life, this tendency to amplify threats can create unnecessary stress and anxiety, making everyday situations feel like high-stakes battles.

When the brain magnifies a problem, it's often attempting to prepare you for the worst-case scenario. It's like a mental rehearsal for disaster. While this might have been useful when faced with life-threatening situations, it becomes problematic when applied to daily challenges, such as a cluttered kitchen or a missed call. The brain's "better safe than sorry" approach leads it to overreact, increasing anxiety and leaving you feeling constantly on edge.

This distortion is further fueled by our emotional state. When we're tired, stressed, or overwhelmed, the brain is more likely to magnify issues because it perceives us as being in a vulnerable state. For instance, if you're already feeling stressed about a work deadline, a minor snag in your evening routine can feel like the tipping point for a full-blown crisis. The brain takes small irritations and inflates them, making them seem like the final straw that will break the camel's back.

Example: Mom Magnifies Bedtime Chaos into a Full-Blown Disaster

ONE THURSDAY NIGHT, I found myself deep in the trenches of what I can only describe as the "Bedtime Apocalypse." The kids had been bouncing off the walls all evening, fueled by a combination of after-dinner cookies and some mysterious source of endless energy. By the time 8:30 p.m. rolled around, I was ready to wind things down. Unfortunately, they had other plans. My daughter was insisting on reading not one but *three* bedtime stories, while my son had suddenly decided it was the perfect moment to test the aerodynamics of every stuffed animal he owned.

As I tried to wrestle them into their pajamas, chaos erupted. My daughter wailed about a missing sock that was "essential" to her sleep, and my son, mid-pajama switch, decided he needed to build a pillow fort *right now*. In my head, I could feel the storm brewing. My brain went into overdrive: "They'll never go to sleep. If they don't sleep, they'll be exhausted tomorrow. They'll be tired and grumpy at school, which will lead to a bad day, and then they'll come home cranky, and we'll go through this all over again! I'm failing as a parent!"

The bedtime chaos grew into what felt like a full-scale war zone. I could see the disaster expanding in my mind: the kids' crankiness tomorrow would lead to chaos at school, which would inevitably reflect poorly on me as a parent. I envisioned a chain reaction of doom that began with tonight's bedtime disaster and ended with my children becoming sleep-deprived wildlings who couldn't function in society. It was all spiraling out of control, and I was convinced that if they didn't settle down soon, the consequences would be nothing short of catastrophic.

By the time my husband peeked into the room, he found me surrounded by pillows, blankets, and half-dressed children, looking like a general who had just lost a crucial battle. He raised an eyebrow and asked cautiously, "How's it going?" I threw up my hands in defeat. "It's a disaster! They won't sleep, and tomorrow is going to be a nightmare!"

Husband's Reassurance: "It's Just Bedtime, Not a World Crisis"

MY HUSBAND, EVER THE calm amidst my self-created storms, chuckled and walked into the room, surveying the scene with the practiced eye of someone who's seen this battle many times before. "It's just bedtime," he said gently, scooping up our daughter to help her find the elusive sock. "Not a world crisis." I glared at him, feeling slightly betrayed by his nonchalance. "But they won't sleep! If they don't sleep, tomorrow will be a disaster!"

He sat down on the floor beside me and began helping our son wriggle into his pajamas. "They'll sleep," he said confidently. "And even if they don't sleep perfectly tonight, it's not the end of the world. One rough night doesn't mean a lifetime of sleep deprivation." I wanted to argue, to point out all the disastrous consequences that awaited us if bedtime didn't go according to plan. But as he calmly navigated the chaos, coaxing our daughter to settle in with her favorite stuffed animal and distracting our son with a story about pirates, I felt my panic start to deflate.

With his reassurance, the situation began to shrink back to its actual size. It was just a hectic bedtime, not a crisis that would determine the rest of our lives. The kids were wild and overtired, but that was par for the course in parenthood. My husband's perspective helped me see that I was magnifying the issue, turning a typical parenting challenge into an imagined catastrophe. Slowly but surely, the kids settled down, lulled into drowsiness by his calm demeanor and steady voice as he read the final story.

As we tiptoed out of their room, I sighed, feeling both relieved and slightly ridiculous. "I really thought this was going to end in total disaster," I admitted. He smiled and put an arm around my shoulders. "It was just bedtime. It's chaotic sometimes, but it's not a doomsday event. Plus, they'll probably sleep in tomorrow, and you'll get a few minutes of peace in the morning." I chuckled, realizing how absurd my catastrophizing had been. In the end, bedtime chaos was just that—chaos, not the end of the world.

5.2 Minimization

MINIMIZATION IS THE opposite side of the catastrophizing coin. While magnification blows problems out of proportion, minimization downplays positive events or qualities, making them seem insignificant. It's the mental habit of brushing off accomplishments with a dismissive "It was no big deal" or thinking that your efforts aren't worth celebrating. This distortion steals the joy and pride you should feel for your successes, convincing you that they don't really matter.

Minimization often disguises itself as humility or modesty, but in reality, it's a refusal to acknowledge the value of your achievements. When you minimize your wins, you deny yourself the sense of accomplishment that comes from recognizing your hard work and progress. Instead of feeling proud, you feel like you're never quite measuring up, constantly dismissing your efforts as not "good enough."

Psychological Explanation of Minimization

MINIMIZATION CAN ARISE from a variety of psychological factors, including a desire to avoid appearing arrogant or the fear of setting high expectations for oneself. Often, people minimize their successes because they don't want to draw attention to themselves or because they believe their achievements are not as significant as those of others. It's a defense mechanism that helps them stay within their comfort zone, avoiding the pressure that comes with recognizing their own worth.

This distortion is also linked to negative self-perception. When someone holds a deep-seated belief that they are not worthy of praise or success, they tend to dismiss their positive qualities and achievements. The brain filters out the positive experiences, reinforcing the belief that they don't deserve recognition. By minimizing their wins, they avoid the discomfort of confronting the possibility that they are, in fact, capable and deserving.

Minimization is further reinforced by societal influences. In a culture that often equates humility with downplaying oneself, many people learn to minimize their achievements as a way to fit in or to avoid making others feel uncomfortable. This habit becomes so ingrained that even when praise is genuinely deserved, it's met with a quick deflection or a shrug, as if success is something that happens by accident rather than as a result of effort and skill.

Example: Mom Downplays Her Outdoor Adventure Skills

LAST MONTH, WE EMBARKED on one of our spontaneous weekend road trips, this time to a remote nature reserve we'd heard about from friends. The place was known for its scenic hiking trails and hidden waterfalls, which immediately sparked my sense of adventure. While I love the outdoors, I'm not exactly the "outdoorsy" type who can navigate through the wilderness with a compass and a strong sense of direction. My husband and I planned to take the kids on a moderate hike—nothing too strenuous, but something that would give them a taste of nature beyond our usual park trips.

On the morning of the hike, I packed a backpack full of essentials: water bottles, snacks, a basic first aid kit, and even a couple of trash bags to clean up after ourselves. We set out, following the trail markers, and before long, found ourselves deep in the forest. The kids were thrilled, picking up sticks and leaves, while Max happily trotted along, occasionally stopping to sniff the air. Halfway through, we came to a fork in the trail with no clear signs pointing us in the right direction. My husband looked at me, his eyes asking, "What's next?"

In that moment, I had a sudden flash of inspiration. Drawing on memories from our road trip days, I decided to lead us off the beaten path toward what looked like a small, unmarked trail. To everyone's surprise, it led us to a secluded clearing with a stunning view of a waterfall cascading down into a crystal-clear pool. It was like stumbling into a hidden paradise. The kids squealed in delight, and even Max seemed to sense the magic of the place, darting around with pure joy.

We spent the afternoon there, skipping rocks, splashing around in the shallow water, and enjoying a picnic by the waterfall. When we finally made our way back to the car, slightly sunburned and thoroughly content, my husband turned to me and said, "You know, you really have a knack for this outdoor stuff. That was amazing!" I felt a swell of pride for a brief moment but quickly brushed it off. "Oh, it was nothing," I replied. "We just got lucky with the trail. Anyone could have found it."

He shook his head, not letting me off the hook. "No, seriously. You took us on an adventure we wouldn't have had if we'd just stuck to the main path. You planned, you led, and you made it happen." But I continued to minimize it. "It was just a hike," I insisted. "I'm not exactly a seasoned explorer."

In my mind, I couldn't see the day as the success it was. I had downplayed my role in navigating us through the woods, discovering a hidden gem, and creating a memorable experience for our family. It wasn't until my daughter, as we were driving home, exclaimed from the back seat, "Mom, you're like an explorer! Can we go on more secret hikes?" that I realized how my minimization was affecting not just how I saw myself but how they saw me. To them, I wasn't just a mom bumbling through the woods—I was a guide on an adventure. And maybe, just maybe, it was time I started seeing it that way too.

Playful Footnote: If Max Can Celebrate His Sock Thefts, Surely We Can Celebrate Our Wins

MAX, OUR RESIDENT SOCK thief, has no problem celebrating his victories. Each time he manages to sneak away with a sock, he parades around the house like he's just won a trophy. There's no minimizing his success—he owns it completely, basking in the glory of his achievement, whether anyone else finds it impressive or not. He doesn't stop to think, "Oh, it's just a sock," or "Well, maybe they didn't hide it very well, so it doesn't count."

Maybe we could all take a page from Max's book. If he can find joy in his small, mischievous victories, why shouldn't we celebrate our own? Life is full of little wins that deserve to be acknowledged, whether it's finishing a big project or simply making it through a hectic day. If Max can revel in his sock-theft triumphs without a hint of doubt, surely we can learn to embrace our accomplishments, no matter how small they may seem.

Chapter 6 Personalization

6.1 Personalization Explained

Personalization is when you take the blame for events that aren't entirely—or even remotely—within your control. It's the mental habit of assuming you're the root cause of every mishap, failure, or bad mood within a 10-mile radius. If the kids have a meltdown in the grocery store, personalization convinces you that it's because of something you did or didn't do, rather than just a normal part of childhood. It's like carrying around a "World's Worst Parent" badge that you pin on yourself at the slightest hint of trouble.

This mindset can be exhausting. You become the emotional manager of not just your own feelings but those of everyone around you. If a family outing goes sideways, it's not just a random series of events—it's a direct reflection of your competence as a parent. You find yourself in a constant state of self-blame, convinced that if you could just do everything perfectly, everyone else would be happy and well-behaved. Spoiler: life doesn't work that way, and neither do kids.

Psychological Explanation of Personalization

PERSONALIZATION ARISES from a deep-seated need to control and make sense of the world. When things go wrong, our brains instinctively look for reasons. It's an old survival mechanism—if our ancestors could identify the cause of a problem, they could potentially avoid it in the future. But in modern life, this mechanism often misfires, leading us to blame ourselves for things that are not our fault. It's an attempt to regain control in situations that feel chaotic or unpredictable.

This cognitive distortion also stems from our desire to be responsible caregivers. As parents, we naturally want the best for our children, and we often measure our success by their behavior. When things don't go as planned, the brain leaps to the conclusion that we must have done something wrong. It's a way of simplifying a complex situation into a single cause-and-effect narrative: "If they're acting out, it must be because of me."

Personalization can also be linked to self-esteem. When someone feels unsure about their abilities, they are more likely to assume that negative outcomes are their fault. This belief creates a feedback loop where every minor issue becomes "evidence" of personal inadequacy. Over time, this can lead to chronic guilt and a skewed perception of reality, where every hiccup is a reflection of one's worth rather than just a part of life's unpredictable nature.

Example: Mom Feels Responsible for Her Kids' Bad Behavior

LAST WEEKEND, WE DECIDED to take the kids to a local art festival. It sounded like the perfect family outing—fresh air, creativity, and a chance for the kids to experience something new. As we wandered through the booths filled with handmade crafts and vibrant paintings, my daughter suddenly decided that she *had* to have a set of glittery, oversized butterfly wings being sold at one of the stands. Meanwhile, my son, who had spotted a booth with toy wooden swords, declared it was his life's mission to become a "knight of the festival."

Before I knew it, we were in the middle of an emotional whirlwind. My daughter, upon learning that the butterfly wings were well beyond our "festival budget," erupted into a dramatic display of tears and wailing. My son, who was denied his knightly aspirations because I wasn't too keen on him wielding a wooden sword around strangers, threw himself onto the ground, shouting about the unfairness of it all. Passersby glanced at us with that mixture of sympathy and judgment that only public child meltdowns can elicit.

In that moment, I felt like the worst parent in the world. Personalization kicked in hard. "This is all my fault," I thought. "I should have known they'd want things and been more prepared. If only I had managed their expectations better, if only I had brought more snacks, if only I had a magic solution for these outbursts." My brain had me convinced that their behavior was a direct reflection of my parenting skills, and I felt the weight of that guilt like a heavy stone in my chest.

As I tried to calm them down, negotiating between butterfly wings and toy swords, I couldn't shake the feeling that I had somehow failed them. To the outside observer, it was a classic case of kids being kids—high hopes dashed by the reality of a parent's wallet and common sense. But in my mind, it was a parenting disaster, and I was the sole architect of the chaos. I carried that feeling home with me, replaying the scene and searching for the moment where I could have "fixed" everything.

Husband's Reminder: "The Kids Are Just Being Kids, Not a Reflection of Your Parenting"

LATER THAT EVENING, after the kids had calmed down and were absorbed in a post-festival movie marathon, I recounted the day's events to my husband. He listened attentively, nodding at the appropriate moments as I described the public meltdowns, the onlookers, and the emotional turmoil I felt. When I finally finished, he looked at me with a mix of empathy and amusement. "You know," he began, "the kids are just being kids. It's not some grand statement about your parenting."

"But they were out of control!" I protested. "And everyone was staring at us like I couldn't handle them." He shrugged. "So what? Kids get upset when they don't get what they want. That's normal. They weren't angry because of something you did wrong. They were just disappointed because they wanted the wings and the sword. If anything, they're learning how to deal with disappointment."

I opened my mouth to argue but found myself at a loss for words. He continued, "Remember when I was a kid and my parents told me I couldn't get that remote-control car? I threw a fit in the middle of the store. My mom still laughs about it, but she never blamed herself. Kids have emotions—they're like little drama machines sometimes. It's not a reflection of you; it's just part of growing up."

His words were like a splash of cold water to the face—refreshing and a bit startling. I had been so caught up in the idea that my kids' public meltdowns were a direct measure of my abilities as a mother that I forgot the simple truth:

children have big feelings, and sometimes those feelings spill over. It wasn't a failure on my part; it was just a moment in their journey of learning how to navigate the world.

He grinned and added, "Plus, if our kids' behavior were really a reflection of us, they'd be the most sarcastic, tech-obsessed, artsy little creatures on the planet. Oh wait..." I laughed, finally letting go of the tension I had been carrying. In the grand scheme of things, the art festival incident was just another episode in the ongoing adventure of parenting. Not a referendum on my skills, but a blip in the unpredictable, sometimes hilarious process of raising kids.

6.2 Letting Go of Responsibility

LETTING GO OF PERSONALIZATION means recognizing that not everything that happens around you is a direct result of your actions. It involves learning to differentiate between what you can control and what is simply out of your hands. When the kids have a meltdown, it's not necessarily because of a parenting flaw—it's just part of their developmental journey. By shifting your perspective, you can begin to see that some things are beyond your influence and not a measure of your worth.

One strategy for letting go of unnecessary responsibility is to take a step back and assess the situation objectively. Ask yourself, "Is this truly something I caused, or is it just a natural part of life?" Often, you'll find that the answer is the latter. Life is full of unpredictable moments, and kids, in particular, are experts at creating chaos for reasons that have nothing to do with parental competence.

Learning to let go also means being kinder to yourself. Recognize that you are doing your best in a world that doesn't always cooperate. Sometimes, the best response to a chaotic situation is to breathe, laugh, and understand that it's not a reflection of your abilities but simply a moment to navigate with grace (or at least as much grace as you can muster while wrangling a preschooler).

Psychological Techniques for Reducing Personalization

TO REDUCE PERSONALIZATION, start by practicing mindfulness. When you feel yourself taking on unnecessary responsibility, pause and observe your thoughts without judgment. Recognize that your brain is jumping to conclusions and gently remind yourself that not everything is about you or within your control. This pause allows you to shift your focus from self-blame to a more balanced understanding of the situation.

Another effective technique is cognitive restructuring. When you catch yourself personalizing an event, challenge the thought by looking for evidence that contradicts it. For instance, if you find yourself thinking, "My child's meltdown is because I'm a bad parent," look for alternative explanations. Is it possible they were tired, hungry, or just having a tough day? By considering other factors, you can break the automatic link between their behavior and your self-worth.

Practice self-compassion. Remind yourself that you are not responsible for everything that happens around you. Acknowledge your feelings of guilt without letting them define you. Treat yourself with the same kindness you would offer a friend. If a friend came to you feeling guilty about their child's behavior, you wouldn't blame them; you'd reassure them that they're a good parent navigating a tough moment. Offer yourself that same reassurance.

Playful Footnote: Max's Sock-Stealing Habit Is Not a Reflection of My Housekeeping Skills

LET'S BE CLEAR—MAX'S sock-stealing habit is not a sign that our home is in disarray. He's a dog with an uncanny ability to find and pilfer socks, no matter how well-hidden they are. It's like he has a sixth sense for laundry baskets. If his antics were truly a reflection of my housekeeping skills, then we'd have to accept that I have a magical sock-stashing gremlin on my hands.

So, when Max proudly prances into the room with a sock dangling from his mouth, it's not a critique of my tidying abilities. It's just Max being Max—joyful, mischievous, and utterly himself. Just like with my kids, not every action that happens in our household is a commentary on my life skills.

Sometimes, a stolen sock is just a stolen sock, and not a symbol of domestic failure.

Chapter 7 Blaming

7.1 Blaming Others

Blaming is the classic escape route when things don't go as planned. It's the mental dodgeball game where you toss the blame to someone else as soon as the pressure builds. In family life, this can look like finding a convenient target whenever chaos ensues. It's the instant reflex to say, "If only you had..." rather than examining the bigger picture. While it might offer a brief sense of relief, blaming ultimately keeps us from addressing the real issues at hand and finding constructive solutions.

In a busy household like ours, where schedules overlap, and unexpected surprises pop up daily, it's easy to fall into the blame trap. The dog didn't get walked? Well, surely someone forgot. The bike is missing a wheel? How could this have happened? Blaming shifts the focus from what we can do next to dwelling on how we got there. It turns ordinary situations into a battleground of fault and defense, missing the opportunity to simply address the matter and move forward.

Psychological Explanation of Blaming

BLAMING OTHERS IS ROOTED in the psychological need to protect our self-esteem and avoid uncomfortable emotions. When something goes awry, pointing fingers at someone else allows us to dodge feelings of guilt, inadequacy, or vulnerability. It's a defense mechanism that deflects the spotlight from our own contributions to a problem, making it easier to preserve our sense of self without facing our shortcomings. This habit is particularly tempting when we're under stress or feeling overwhelmed, as it provides a quick, though temporary, relief from internal conflict.

The human brain is wired to seek explanations for negative events. By assigning blame to someone else, we simplify the situation, creating a clear cause-and-effect narrative. This can make us feel like we've regained control, even if it's at the expense of harmony or personal growth. Blaming others also aligns with our natural tendency to view ourselves more favorably, a bias that helps maintain our self-image but can hinder honest self-assessment.

In the long run, blaming others can become a barrier to personal growth and healthy relationships. It prevents us from looking inward and recognizing our own role in situations. Without this self-awareness, we miss the chance to learn and improve. Moreover, a culture of blame can create tension within families or teams, fostering defensiveness rather than cooperation. It shifts the focus from solving problems to avoiding fault, which rarely leads to positive outcomes.

Example: Mom Blames Her Husband for the "Great Garden Showdown"

LAST SUMMER, WE DECIDED to try our hand at a small backyard garden. My husband, who has a particular fondness for tech gadgets, was in charge of setting up an automatic watering system. I, on the other hand, took on the task of selecting and planting the flowers and herbs, with the kids eagerly helping to dig holes and scatter seeds. It was supposed to be our little oasis, a peaceful project to enjoy as a family. That was the plan, anyway.

Weeks went by, and for a while, everything seemed to be going smoothly. The kids were excited to see their tiny seedlings sprouting, and Max had taken to patrolling the garden like it was his personal domain. Then, one sweltering afternoon, I stepped outside to find half the garden looking wilted and forlorn. The flowers were drooping, the herbs were crispy, and our once-promising patch of green had turned into a sun-scorched battlefield. I felt a wave of frustration wash over me. This was not the serene garden I had envisioned.

My immediate reaction was to find the source of the problem, and my eyes zeroed in on the watering system. I marched back inside and found my husband tinkering with one of his gadgets. "Did you even check the watering system?" I blurted out, barely concealing my annoyance. He looked up, surprised. "I thought it was set to water every morning," he replied, a bit defensively. "Well, it's not working," I snapped. "The garden looks like a disaster zone! If you had just checked it more often, maybe we wouldn't be in this mess."

He put down his gadget and followed me outside. After a quick inspection, he pointed out that a few of the sprinkler heads had been knocked out of place—likely by Max during one of his patrols. Suddenly, the situation was less about his supposed negligence and more about a combination of factors: an overly eager dog, some technical mishaps, and perhaps a bit of oversight on both our parts. But in that heated moment, I had jumped straight into the blame game, casting him as the sole villain in the "Great Garden Showdown."

Playful Scene: Kids Laugh as Parents Lightheartedly Argue About Who's to Blame

THE KIDS HAD BEEN OBSERVING our garden fiasco from the kitchen window. As we knelt down to adjust the sprinkler heads, they came outside, curiosity written all over their faces. "What happened to the flowers?" my daughter asked, her brow furrowed. I hesitated, about to launch into a recount of the malfunctioning watering system, but my husband beat me to it.

"Well," he began, with a mischievous grin, "it seems our garden guardian, Max, has been a little too enthusiastic in his duties." He gestured towards Max, who was now lounging under the shade, blissfully unaware of the trouble he'd caused. The kids giggled at the sight of Max, their beloved sock-thief-turned-garden-trampler.

"Wait," my son interjected, pointing at the sprinklers. "Didn't you say you set these up so we wouldn't have to water every day?" My husband chuckled, giving me a sideways glance. "Ah, yes, the wonders of modern technology. But it seems even technology needs a helping hand now and then." He turned to me and added with a wink, "And maybe a bit more supervision."

I couldn't help but laugh. Here we were, a team of overambitious gardeners blaming each other—and the dog—for a situation that was, in truth, a collective experiment gone slightly awry. The kids joined in our banter, playfully pointing out how each of us had contributed to the garden's downfall. "Mom picked flowers that need a lot of water," my daughter teased. "And Dad said the sprinklers would do all the work," my son chimed in. It became a lighthearted family debate, filled with more laughter than blame.

We spent the rest of the afternoon working together to revive the garden. The kids helped adjust the sprinklers, my husband tweaked the settings, and I made a mental note to choose more drought-resistant plants next time. As we worked, the finger-pointing faded, replaced by the realization that we were all part of this little backyard adventure—triumphs and mishaps included.

7.2 Taking Responsibility

TAKING RESPONSIBILITY means moving past the instinct to blame and instead focusing on what can be done to address the issue at hand. It requires acknowledging that life is rarely as simple as one person's fault. By embracing the complexity of situations, we open the door to collaboration and problem-solving. In our garden scenario, it wasn't about who failed but about what we could learn and how we could work together to create something beautiful.

Recognizing when blame is taking over involves mindfulness and a willingness to pause before reacting. Instead of jumping to conclusions, take a moment to assess the situation. Ask yourself, "What part did I play in this?" and "What can we do now to improve things?" This shift from blaming to taking responsibility encourages a more proactive and positive approach to life's challenges.

Accepting responsibility doesn't mean taking the blame for everything. It means being honest about your role and considering how you can contribute to a solution. It fosters a sense of ownership and agency, transforming setbacks into opportunities for growth and learning.

Psychological Techniques for Reducing Blaming

A USEFUL TECHNIQUE for reducing the urge to blame is to practice empathy. Before pointing fingers, consider the perspectives of everyone involved. In the garden example, understanding my husband's reliance on the automated system and Max's playful nature helped me see the situation from a broader viewpoint. Empathy allows you to see the nuances in situations rather than jumping to black-and-white conclusions.

Another strategy is to frame challenges as collective experiences rather than individual failures. Instead of thinking, "You didn't fix the sprinklers," shift to, "Our garden needs some attention." This language change moves the focus from assigning fault to working together toward a solution. It reinforces the idea that, as a family or team, you're all in it together.

Lastly, use humor to defuse tension. Lightheartedly acknowledging the mishap, as we did with the kids, can turn a blaming session into a bonding moment. It's a reminder that life is full of unexpected turns, and sometimes, it's more about how we respond than who's to blame.

Playful Footnote: If Max Can Own Up to His Sock Thefts (Which He Never Does), We Can Take Responsibility Too

MAX'S SOCK-STEALING escapades are the epitome of guilt-free living. He waltzes into the room with a sock in his mouth, eyes gleaming with mischief, and if he could speak, you just know he'd say, "Yep, I did it. So what?" There's no blame game in Max's world—just unfiltered joy in his actions.

While we may not want to emulate his brazen disregard for sock ownership, there's a lesson in his confidence. Taking responsibility doesn't mean wallowing in blame; it means acknowledging our actions with the same unapologetic honesty. If Max can parade his "crimes" without an ounce of shame, surely we can own up to our contributions to life's little messes with a bit of grace and humor.

Chapter 8 Labeling

8.1 Self-Labeling

Labeling is the mental habit of attaching a fixed label to oneself or others based on a single event or characteristic. It's like taking one piece of the puzzle and assuming it defines the entire picture. When someone makes a mistake, they might label themselves as "a failure," ignoring the vast range of their abilities and experiences. These labels can become a heavy emotional burden, boxing us into a narrow view of who we are.

This tendency to label can distort our perception, turning momentary lapses into permanent identities. For instance, tripping up in a social setting might lead someone to label themselves as "awkward" or "socially inept," even though everyone has clumsy moments. Labels simplify the complexity of our identities into one-dimensional tags, creating an internal narrative that can be hard to shake off.

Psychological Explanation of Labeling

LABELING STEMS FROM the brain's need to make sense of the world in simple terms. Humans are wired to categorize information quickly, helping us navigate social dynamics and understand our surroundings. While this ability to label can be helpful in certain contexts, like identifying a "friendly face" in a crowd, it becomes problematic when applied rigidly to ourselves or others. It narrows our self-perception and leads to a fixed mindset, where one mistake becomes a definitive statement about our character.

Labeling can also be a defense mechanism. By assigning a label, we attempt to make an uncomfortable situation more predictable. For example, if you fumble during a presentation and label yourself as "terrible at public speaking," it offers a sense of closure. However, this closure comes at the cost of limiting your self-view and potential for growth. It prevents us from seeing mistakes as isolated events and instead turns them into evidence of a "flawed" identity.

This distortion can result in an ongoing cycle of self-criticism. When we label ourselves negatively, we become more sensitive to situations that reinforce that label. If you've labeled yourself as "clumsy," every stumble, however minor, becomes a confirmation of that identity. The brain selectively focuses on instances that align with the label, ignoring the countless times when you navigated the world just fine. Over time, the label solidifies, making it harder to see yourself as anything but that limiting definition.

Example: "The Crafty Catastrophe"

A FEW MONTHS AGO, I decided to join a local community art project. It was an outdoor mural that would eventually adorn the side of a historic building downtown. As someone who enjoys creative projects, I was excited to contribute. My husband and the kids cheered me on, imagining a world where their mom was secretly the next Picasso. I envisioned a scene of harmonious painting, contributing my little part to a grand, collective masterpiece.

The project began on a sunny Saturday, with volunteers of all ages gathered around the massive canvas. My designated section was a small patch meant to depict a whimsical garden. Armed with brushes and paint, I dove in, blending colors and adding playful swirls. About an hour into the project, things took a turn. In my enthusiasm, I knocked over a can of bright blue paint. It splashed everywhere, leaving a splatter pattern that extended far beyond my patch of garden. I stood there, brush in hand, as fellow volunteers turned to see the unexpected burst of "art" I had just added to their mural.

In that moment, a label flashed in my mind: "Clumsy Artist." I felt a rush of embarrassment. This was supposed to be a moment of community and creativity, and here I was, accidentally tie-dyeing the mural with unintended paint splatters. As others quickly rushed in with rags and good-natured laughter, I was already sinking into a mental loop. "Why do I always mess things up?" I thought. "I shouldn't have volunteered. I'm clearly not cut out for this."

Despite the volunteers' reassurances and the project's organizers joking that my "blue burst" added a dynamic element to the mural, I couldn't shake off the self-label. For the rest of the day, I hesitated with every brushstroke, second-guessing my every move. In my mind, I was no longer part of the artistic community effort. I was "the one who spilled paint."

Humorous Footnote: The Accidental Abstract Artist

INTERESTINGLY, MY BLUE paint catastrophe gained a bit of local fame. The mural was later featured in a community newsletter with a caption that read, "Volunteers add unexpected flair to downtown mural!" accompanied by a picture of my accidental splash. My husband, always quick with humor, suggested that I embrace my new artistic style—"Abstract Accidentalism." He even joked about hosting a gallery opening featuring "works by the renowned accidental artist who challenges the boundaries of traditional brush control."

While I couldn't help but laugh, it was a reminder that sometimes our labels—whether serious or playful—are simply one part of a larger story. In this case, my "catastrophe" became a unique, if unintended, contribution to the mural. Maybe it wasn't about being a "clumsy artist" after all. Perhaps, in the grand scheme, I was just adding my own splash of color to the world.

8.2 Moving Beyond Labels

MOVING BEYOND LABELS involves recognizing that no single event or trait defines who we are. We are complex beings with a wide range of abilities, experiences, and emotions. By letting go of rigid labels, we open ourselves up to a more nuanced and compassionate view of our identities. Instead of seeing ourselves through the lens of a single mishap, we learn to appreciate the multifaceted nature of who we are.

One way to break free from labels is to reframe the language we use about ourselves. Instead of saying, "I'm clumsy," shift to, "I had a clumsy moment." This small change in phrasing acknowledges the event without turning it into a defining characteristic. It creates room for growth and change, allowing us to see our actions as part of a larger, more dynamic self.

By recognizing that labels are often self-imposed limitations, we can begin to challenge them. Ask yourself, "Is this label serving me, or is it holding me back?"

Often, you'll find that labels do more harm than good. They keep us boxed into a narrow view of ourselves, preventing us from exploring new possibilities and embracing our full potential.

Psychological Techniques for Reducing Labeling

A HELPFUL TECHNIQUE for reducing labeling is to practice self-distancing. When you catch yourself using a label, step back and look at the situation objectively. Ask, "If this happened to a friend, would I label them the same way?" Often, you'll find that you wouldn't be nearly as harsh on someone else as you are on yourself. This perspective shift helps you see the event as a single occurrence rather than a defining moment.

Another effective strategy is to focus on specific actions rather than overarching labels. Instead of saying, "I'm a failure," identify what specifically went wrong and consider what you can learn from it. For example, "I knocked over the paint can" is a factual statement that doesn't carry the weight of a self-label. By concentrating on actions, you can address them constructively without internalizing them as part of your identity.

Practicing self-compassion is also crucial. Acknowledge that everyone makes mistakes and that these moments don't diminish your worth. Remind yourself that you are more than any single event or trait. Cultivating a mindset of self-kindness helps break the cycle of negative labeling, replacing it with a more balanced and forgiving view of yourself.

Conversation: "A Family Portrait of Labels"

ONE EVENING, AFTER the mural incident had become a humorous family anecdote, we decided to do something different during our usual game night. My husband proposed an exercise: we would each share a label we've assigned to ourselves and then have the family offer an alternative perspective. At first, the kids thought it was a strange game, but they quickly got on board.

I started, sharing my "clumsy artist" label from the mural project. My daughter looked at me with a serious expression. "Mom, you're not clumsy. You just made the mural more fun!" My son added, "Yeah, it needed more blue anyway." Their innocent logic made me laugh. They saw the incident not as a failure, but as a playful addition to the artwork. My husband chimed in, "See? To them, you're not a clumsy artist. You're a bold creator of unexpected masterpieces."

Then it was my husband's turn. He labeled himself as "Mr. Fix-It," always feeling responsible for fixing things around the house and feeling like a failure when he couldn't. The kids protested immediately. "Dad, you're not just Mr. Fix-It," my daughter said. "You're also Mr. Fun Games and Mr. Cool Gadgets." My son nodded vigorously. "Yeah, and Mr. Best Pancakes!" My husband grinned. "I guess I am more than just a repairman."

The exercise became a lighthearted way to challenge our self-imposed labels. It showed us how the labels we place on ourselves are often far harsher than how others see us. Through their eyes, our so-called failures were reimagined as contributions to the family story—a story filled with creativity, fun, and, yes, the occasional splash of paint.

Humorous Footnote: Max, The "Sock Bandit"

MAX, IN HIS INFINITE wisdom, has never labeled himself. If he had to pick one, though, it would probably be something along the lines of "Sock Bandit Extraordinaire." He embraces his identity with zero shame. Each stolen sock is a triumph, not a testament to his "mischievous" nature. He parades around with his prize as if to say, "I am Max, the Great Sock Bandit, and this is my kingdom!"

Perhaps we could take a cue from Max. Rather than assigning ourselves restrictive labels, we could simply embrace our quirks and occasional blunders as part of the rich tapestry of who we are. After all, life is far more interesting with a little bit of unpredictability—and maybe, a sock or two out of place.

Chapter 9 Always Being Right

9.1 The Need to Be Right

The need to always be right is a cognitive distortion that sneaks into everyday interactions. It's the feeling that every discussion is a debate you must win, and every opinion you hold is the hill you're willing to die on. Whether it's a minor disagreement about the best way to fold laundry or a more serious debate over the correct lyrics to a 90s rock song, the need to be right can turn even the smallest things into a battlefield. It often leads to frustration, defensiveness, and a whole lot of unnecessary tension.

In a family setting, this need can rear its head in the most unexpected places. It's the instinct to correct a child's innocent misconception or to argue over the exact name of the dinosaur that used to reside in the natural history museum. When everyone's striving to be the "right one," the fun can quickly drain from a conversation, replaced by a stubborn standoff that leaves everyone feeling a bit more irritable and a lot less connected.

Psychological Explanation of the Need to Be Right

THE NEED TO ALWAYS be right often stems from deeper psychological roots, such as insecurity or the fear of being seen as inadequate. For many, being right provides a sense of control and safety in a world that can feel unpredictable and chaotic. It's a mental defense mechanism—a way to build a protective wall around one's self-esteem. If you're right, then you're competent, knowledgeable, and, most importantly, not vulnerable to criticism or judgment.

This cognitive distortion can also develop from past experiences where being wrong led to negative consequences, like ridicule or punishment. Over time, the brain learns to equate being right with being safe. It becomes a way to avoid the discomfort that comes with making mistakes or admitting gaps in knowledge. Always striving to be right becomes less about the actual correctness and more about avoiding the emotional fallout of being wrong.

However, this need can strain relationships and limit personal growth. When the focus is solely on being right, conversations become a quest for validation rather than an exchange of ideas. The brain gets locked into a defensive mode, where every statement is a potential threat to one's sense of competence. This mindset closes off the possibility of learning from others, reducing opportunities for deeper connections and mutual understanding.

Example: "The Grand Kite Debacle"

ONE BREEZY SATURDAY afternoon, we decided it would be a fantastic idea to take the kids to the park and fly kites. The sky was a brilliant blue, and the wind conditions seemed just right. My husband, ever the tech enthusiast, had ordered a high-tech kite that promised "superior aerodynamics" and "precision control." Meanwhile, I had picked out a simpler, more classic kite with a rainbow tail, the kind that relied more on sheer luck than advanced engineering. As we approached the park, we could already feel the seeds of a subtle competition being sown.

After a few minutes of assembling the kites, we were ready for takeoff. My husband went first, carefully unfurling the string and adjusting the controls on his "super kite." The kids watched in awe as he executed precise maneuvers, launching the kite smoothly into the air. It was a picture-perfect moment—until the wind decided to throw in a curveball. His kite veered sharply to the left, diving toward the ground in a series of chaotic loops. "It's the wind direction," he muttered, adjusting the controls furiously. "It's just not stable enough for advanced flight patterns."

Seeing my opportunity, I stepped forward with my humble, rainbow-tailed kite. "Maybe it just needs a simpler approach," I said, not so subtly implying that perhaps my kite was better suited for the task. I let out the string and, with a light tug, my kite began to rise. It caught the wind and floated gently upwards, twisting gracefully in the sky. "See," I started to say, "sometimes less is more—" But just as the words left my mouth, my kite performed an unexpected somersault and plummeted straight into a nearby tree.

For a split second, there was silence. Then, with a slight smirk, my husband turned to me. "Superior aerodynamics, huh?" he teased, echoing my earlier tone. "Well," I stammered, searching for a reason why my kite's nosedive wasn't a failure. "The tree...it was in the way. And maybe this kite isn't meant for sudden gusts." We both stood there, kites tangled and fallen, clinging to our need to be right about whose approach to kite flying was superior.

Playful Footnote: The Philosophical Debate of the Fallen Kites

LATER, AS WE SAT ON the grass untangling our kites, it struck me how comical the whole situation was. What started as a simple family outing had morphed into a pseudo-philosophical debate about aerodynamics and wind patterns. My husband jokingly suggested that we write a paper: "The Grand Kite Debate: When High-Tech Meets Nostalgia in the Sky." We laughed at the absurdity of it all. The kids, meanwhile, were far more interested in using the fallen kites as makeshift capes for an impromptu superhero game.

In the end, the park had witnessed not a battle of engineering versus simplicity, but rather two adults wrestling with their need to prove they were right—even when it was about something as whimsical as flying kites. The sky might not have been filled with our soaring kites that day, but it certainly was filled with laughter.

9.2 Accepting Mistakes

ACCEPTING MISTAKES is a liberating experience. It allows for more meaningful interactions, free from the pressure to constantly defend one's correctness. When we let go of the need to be right, conversations become opportunities to learn and connect rather than contests to win. This shift not only reduces emotional strain but also opens the door to a richer, more varied understanding of the world and the people in it.

In the context of relationships, embracing the possibility of being wrong can be incredibly enriching. It shows a willingness to be vulnerable and to prioritize connection over ego. When we admit, "I might be wrong," we invite others into a space of mutual respect and open dialogue. This, in turn, fosters a sense of trust and understanding, building a more supportive environment for everyone involved.

Psychological Techniques for Letting Go of Being Right

ONE EFFECTIVE TECHNIQUE for letting go of the need to be right is to practice mindfulness. When you feel the urge to defend your correctness, pause and observe your thoughts. Notice the defensiveness rising within you and question its origin. Often, the need to be right is driven by a deeper fear of being judged or not being good enough. By acknowledging this fear, you can respond to the situation with more compassion and less rigidity.

Another helpful strategy is to cultivate a sense of curiosity. Instead of focusing on proving your point, shift your mindset to learning from the other person's perspective. Ask open-ended questions and listen actively. This approach transforms disagreements into learning opportunities, where being wrong is not a defeat but a chance to broaden your understanding. Over time, this practice can help you see that being right is not the ultimate goal—genuine connection is.

Lastly, embrace the idea of "beginner's mind," a concept from Zen Buddhism that encourages approaching situations with an open and eager mindset, free of preconceived notions. By adopting this attitude, you allow yourself to be a learner rather than an expert. It fosters humility and flexibility, making it easier to accept that your perspective is just one of many possible viewpoints.

Conversation: "The Value of Being Wrong"

ONE EVENING, AFTER the kite debacle had become a running joke in our family, my husband and I sat down for a casual chat about our mutual obsession with being right. "You know," he started, "that kite situation was ridiculous. Why do we care so much about being right, even about something as trivial as kite flying?" I laughed, nodding. "I guess it's because we're both stubborn. But I have to admit, it was pretty funny in hindsight."

He smiled. "What if we tried an experiment? What if, for the next week, we make a point of admitting when we're wrong—about anything, no matter how small?" I raised an eyebrow, intrigued by the challenge. "You mean, like a 'Wrong Week'?" He nodded. "Exactly. Let's see what happens when we let go of being right for a while."

We agreed to the experiment, and it led to some hilarious moments. The next day, I confidently declared that the new song playing on the radio was by a certain artist. My husband corrected me gently, and instead of arguing, I threw up my hands and said, "Oops, I was wrong!" We both burst out laughing at how freeing it felt to just admit it. Later, he misjudged the amount of time it would take to get to a movie theater. As we arrived late, he turned to me with a grin and said, "Yep, I was wrong about the timing." It became a running gag, defusing situations that might otherwise have led to bickering.

The experiment revealed that admitting we were wrong didn't diminish us in each other's eyes. In fact, it made our interactions lighter and more honest. It was a reminder that being wrong wasn't a failure—it was a part of being human. By the end of "Wrong Week," we had accumulated a list of laughable errors, each serving as a testament to the freedom that comes with letting go of the need to always be right.

Humorous Footnote: "Max Never Thinks He's Wrong, but He's Probably Right About That"

MAX, IN HIS CANINE wisdom, has never once doubted his decisions. If he steals a sock, it's because that sock clearly belonged in his mouth. If he digs a hole in the garden, well, it's because the universe obviously needed that hole. Max operates in a world where he is perpetually right, and the rest of us just haven't caught up with his genius yet.

While we might not want to adopt Max's unwavering self-assurance in every aspect of life, there's something to be said for his confidence. Perhaps the lesson here is that sometimes, it's not about being right or wrong—it's about living with a sense of joy and curiosity, even when we end up tangled in our own metaphorical kite strings.

Chapter 10 Should Statements

10.1 The Trap of "Should"

"Should" statements are like the uninvited guests at a party, always telling you how things ought to be while ignoring the reality of the situation. They impose rigid expectations, like an invisible rulebook dictating what you and everyone around you are supposed to do. Whether it's the idea that you should always be on top of your game or that your kids should behave perfectly in public, these statements often lead to feelings of guilt, disappointment, and an ever-present sense of falling short.

In family life, "should" statements sneak into the daily routine in the most mundane moments. You might catch yourself thinking, "I should be able to juggle work, parenting, and personal time effortlessly," or "My kids should always be polite and well-mannered." These internalized rules create an impossible standard, turning every little misstep into a perceived failure. Instead of embracing the beautiful messiness of life, we get caught in the trap of "should."

Psychological Explanation of "Should" Statements

THE USE OF "SHOULD" statements often stems from internalized beliefs and societal expectations that have been ingrained over time. These statements create a set of rules in our minds—rules that are often unrealistic and inflexible. They act as mental guidelines that dictate how things "ought" to be, leaving little room for imperfection or the natural ebb and flow of life. By holding ourselves and others to these rigid standards, we inadvertently set up a cycle of pressure and guilt.

"Should" statements also serve as a way to control and make sense of our environment. By adhering to these internal rules, we try to impose order on the chaos of life. It gives a false sense of control, as if by following these self-imposed "laws," we can guarantee a specific outcome. Unfortunately, life rarely conforms to these expectations, leading to frustration when things don't go as planned. Instead of offering control, "should" statements often leave us feeling powerless and inadequate.

This cognitive distortion becomes a mental trap, causing a person to view life through a lens of constant judgment. When the focus is on how things should be rather than how they are, there's little room for compassion or acceptance. This judgmental mindset prevents us from seeing the present moment clearly and appreciating the nuances of each situation. It turns every deviation from the "rules" into a failure, reinforcing a negative self-image and preventing us from embracing life's imperfections.

Example: "The Neighborhood Talent Show Saga"

EVERY SUMMER, OUR NEIGHBORHOOD hosts a talent show. It's a lighthearted event where kids, parents, and even pets get a chance to showcase their hidden (or not-so-hidden) talents. Last year, my daughter decided she wanted to perform a magic act, inspired by a magician we had seen during a family outing. I was thrilled by her enthusiasm and immediately found myself slipping into "should" mode. "I should help her prepare the best magic act this neighborhood has ever seen," I thought. "She should amaze everyone."

We spent weeks practicing. My husband and I took turns playing the audience while she rehearsed her tricks. My son even acted as her stage assistant, mostly because he liked the idea of disappearing behind a curtain. But as the day of the talent show approached, my "should" statements multiplied. "She should have the perfect costume," I insisted, so we spent an afternoon sewing sequins onto an old cape. "She should have flawless timing," I decided, so we practiced her routine over and over.

On the evening of the talent show, the neighborhood gathered in the community center. Kids lined up to perform, from piano solos to dance routines. When it was finally my daughter's turn, I felt a knot of nervous excitement in my stomach. She took the stage confidently, her cape sparkling under the lights. She began her routine with grace, but midway through, her big finale trick—a "disappearing scarf"—didn't go as planned. The scarf stubbornly refused to vanish and instead clung to her hand. There was an awkward silence before she shrugged, grinned at the audience, and said, "Ta-da?"

The crowd erupted in laughter, and they applauded her bravery. She took a bow, looking both relieved and slightly embarrassed. But in that moment, all I could think was, "She should have been flawless. I should have helped her more. This shouldn't have happened." I was so wrapped up in my "should" statements that I almost missed the bigger picture: the audience's admiration for her willingness to perform and her ability to laugh at herself.

My daughter, however, didn't seem fazed. As she came off the stage, she beamed and said, "That was fun! Did you see how they laughed?" I managed a smile, realizing that while my "should" statements had made this talent show a high-stakes performance in my mind, for her, it was simply a moment to try something new and enjoy the process.

Humorous Footnote: "I Should Also Be Able to Stop Max from Stealing Socks, But We See How That's Going"

LET'S BE REAL: IF WE applied "should" statements to every aspect of life, Max should have ceased his sock-stealing antics ages ago. I should have been able to train him to resist the allure of unattended laundry. Yet here we are, with Max prancing through the living room with a sock in his mouth like it's a trophy. Some things in life defy the "shoulds," and perhaps that's a reminder that flexibility often serves us better than rigid expectations.

Maybe it's not about stopping Max from his beloved pastime but rather accepting that some things—and dogs—simply have their own way of being. "Should" statements have a way of making us feel responsible for the uncontrollable, but sometimes, it's better to just let the socks be and laugh at the little absurdities they bring.

10.2 Replacing "Should" with Preferences

REPLACING "SHOULD" with preferences is a gentle shift in perspective. Instead of imposing rigid rules, it involves expressing what we would like to happen in a way that allows room for flexibility. Rather than saying, "I should be more organized," try, "I would prefer to be more organized." This subtle change opens up a space for self-compassion, acknowledging desires without the weight of obligation.

This approach helps reduce feelings of failure and disappointment. It acknowledges that while we may have certain goals or ideals, they are not demands that we must fulfill to prove our worth. Preferences allow us to navigate life with more grace, recognizing that there are many ways to experience success and fulfillment.

Psychological Techniques for Replacing "Should" with More Compassionate Language

ONE EFFECTIVE TECHNIQUE is to catch yourself in the act of using "should" statements and reframe them as preferences. When you notice a "should" thought, pause and ask yourself, "What would I prefer instead?" For example, if you think, "I should be more patient with the kids," rephrase it as, "I would prefer to be more patient with the kids." This subtle change shifts the tone from self-criticism to a more understanding and supportive mindset.

Another strategy is to practice self-compassion. When you find yourself using "should" statements, take a moment to acknowledge that you are doing your best in a complex world. Remind yourself that life is full of unpredictable variables, and it's okay not to have everything perfectly aligned. This practice helps break the cycle of guilt and pressure that "should" statements often create.

Lastly, try replacing "should" with "could" or "might." These words imply possibility rather than obligation. For instance, instead of saying, "I should finish this project tonight," try, "I could finish this project tonight if I have the energy." This language change introduces flexibility and allows you to consider other factors, such as your well-being, without feeling like you're letting yourself down.

Conversation: "The Great Superhero Debate"

ONE EVENING, DURING a family game of charades, the topic of superheroes came up. My son insisted that Batman should be able to fly because, in his words, "He's Batman! He should do everything!" My husband, taking his role as the resident comic book expert quite seriously, countered, "Actually, Batman isn't supposed to fly; he uses gadgets and his intelligence. That's what makes him different."

As they launched into a lighthearted debate about superhero abilities, I caught myself thinking, "I should step in and clarify this. They should understand the actual comic lore." But then I paused. What if I reframed this moment not as an opportunity to enforce my "shoulds" but as a chance to simply enjoy their imaginative discussion?

So instead of intervening, I added to the fun. "Or maybe," I chimed in, "Batman could fly if he invented a jet-powered cape." The kids' eyes widened at the thought. "Yes!" my daughter exclaimed. "A jet-powered cape that also shoots confetti!" My son nodded in agreement, completely abandoning his original "should" stance in favor of this new, wildly creative idea.

In the end, the conversation wasn't about who was right or what Batman "should" be able to do. It was about exploring possibilities and enjoying each other's company. The "shoulds" melted away, replaced by laughter and the boundless creativity that only comes when you let go of rigid expectations.

Humorous Footnote: "Max Would Prefer If We Said He 'Prefers Socks' Instead of 'Steals Socks'—Language Matters"

MAX WOULD PROBABLY argue that he doesn't "steal" socks. In his world, he simply has a strong preference for them. If he could speak, he'd likely insist that we reframe the narrative: "Max prefers to collect socks as part of his personal treasure trove." And perhaps there's a lesson there. Maybe it's not about the rigid labels we place on actions but about understanding the underlying preferences that drive them.

So, the next time I catch Max trotting away with yet another sock, I might just remind myself that he's not breaking any "should" rules. He's simply expressing a preference—albeit a sock-centric one—and teaching us all a lesson in embracing our quirks without the heavy burden of "should."

Chapter 11 Emotional Reasoning

11.1 Emotions as Truths

Emotional reasoning is the mental process where feelings are taken as absolute truths. If you feel anxious, you assume something bad is about to happen. If you feel guilty, you believe you must have done something wrong. This cognitive distortion convinces you that your emotional state reflects reality, even when there's little evidence to support it. In family life, emotional reasoning can lead to unnecessary worry, misunderstandings, and moments of tension that aren't rooted in the facts of a situation.

This tendency can sneak into daily life in surprising ways. It's that gut feeling of inadequacy during a casual conversation, leading you to believe that everyone around you must think the same. Or it's the wave of irritation after a long day that makes you feel like the universe is conspiring against you. The danger of emotional reasoning lies in how it turns fleeting emotions into supposed facts, distorting the view of reality.

Psychological Explanation of Emotional Reasoning

EMOTIONAL REASONING stems from the brain's natural inclination to prioritize emotions as indicators of danger or safety. This cognitive process is part of the human survival mechanism—our emotions often signal how we should react to certain situations. However, when emotions become the primary lens through which we interpret the world, they can overshadow logic and reason. This is why emotional reasoning feels so convincing; it taps into our instinctive need to trust our feelings as guides.

Emotions, while valuable, are not always accurate reflections of reality. They are influenced by a variety of factors, including past experiences, mood, and even physical states like fatigue or hunger. Emotional reasoning takes these subjective feelings and falsely elevates them to the status of objective truths. For example, feeling anxious about an upcoming event can lead to the conclusion that something bad will happen, even if there's no concrete evidence to support that belief.

This cognitive distortion also has a self-perpetuating nature. When we rely on emotions to determine truth, we often look for information that confirms those feelings, ignoring evidence that contradicts them. This selective perception reinforces emotional reasoning, making it difficult to see beyond the emotional fog. Over time, it can lead to a cycle where feelings, rather than facts, dictate our actions and decisions.

Example: "The Mystery of the Missing Remote"

ONE EVENING, AFTER a long day, I was looking forward to a bit of downtime with my family. My husband had set up our living room for a movie night, complete with popcorn and cozy blankets. As we gathered around the couch, I noticed something crucial was missing—the remote. Now, in our household, the remote has a mysterious way of vanishing just when it's needed most. This time was no exception.

We began the ritual of searching for the elusive remote. Cushions were lifted, blankets shaken, and yet, it was nowhere to be found. As the minutes ticked by, I felt a wave of frustration rising within me. "It's always like this," I thought. "Why can't we ever keep track of one simple thing?" My annoyance quickly morphed into a sense of dread. My emotions were leading me to a dramatic conclusion: our entire evening was ruined.

In that moment, emotional reasoning took over. "If I feel this frustrated," I reasoned, "then it must mean something is wrong. We're clearly too disorganized as a family. This is why we can never have a smooth, relaxing evening." My emotions spiraled, turning a small inconvenience into a supposed indication of a larger, underlying problem with our household.

Meanwhile, my husband continued the search, calmly checking behind furniture and inside drawers. The kids, sensing the growing tension, joined in with their own search tactics—my son attempted to "use the Force" to summon the remote, while my daughter, armed with a flashlight, declared herself the "Remote Detective." In the midst of this hunt, I was still stuck in my emotional reasoning, convinced that this was more than just a lost remote; it was a symbol of our failure to manage even the simplest of tasks.

Just as I was about to give up and declare the evening a failure, Max trotted into the room with his tail wagging. In his mouth, of course, was the remote. He had apparently found it during his earlier adventures and decided it made a good chew toy. The whole room burst into laughter, and I was snapped out of my emotional fog. In reality, it was just a silly mishap, not an omen of a dysfunctional family life.

Playful Footnote: "Trusting Your Emotions with Max's Guidance"

MAX SEEMS TO LIVE HIS life in a state of emotional reasoning bliss. If he feels like a sock thief, then he is a sock thief, and nothing can convince him otherwise. In his world, emotions are facts, and if the mood strikes him to parade around with a remote in his mouth, then that's simply the reality of the moment. Perhaps there's a lesson here in not taking our emotions too seriously, especially when they lead us to conclusions that are as absurd as believing a missing remote is the end of family harmony.

Maybe next time, I'll take a page out of Max's book and remember that feelings are not always the final word. Sometimes, they're just the background noise to a hilarious, unexpected turn of events.

11.2 Challenging Emotional Reasoning

CHALLENGING EMOTIONAL reasoning requires a conscious effort to separate feelings from facts. It means recognizing that emotions are valid but not always accurate reflections of reality. By questioning the conclusions drawn from emotions, we can begin to see situations more clearly and respond in a way that is balanced rather than reactive. This shift allows for a healthier, more grounded approach to life's ups and downs.

The goal is not to dismiss or invalidate feelings but to understand that they are one piece of a larger puzzle. By acknowledging emotions without letting them dictate our perception of reality, we create space for more thoughtful responses.

This practice reduces the emotional turbulence that comes from assuming our feelings are the sole truth.

Psychological Strategies for Separating Emotions from Reality

ONE EFFECTIVE STRATEGY for challenging emotional reasoning is to practice mindfulness. When emotions start to take over, pause and observe them without judgment. Notice what you're feeling and how those emotions are influencing your thoughts. This mindfulness creates a mental space where you can question the validity of your emotional conclusions. Ask yourself, "Is this feeling based on facts, or is it a reaction to a specific situation?"

Another technique is to seek evidence that either supports or contradicts your emotional reasoning. For example, if you're feeling like a failure because of a minor setback, take a moment to list other instances where you've succeeded. This evidence-based approach helps to counterbalance the emotional narrative with factual information, providing a more realistic perspective.

Cognitive reframing is also a useful tool. When caught in emotional reasoning, reframe the situation in a way that acknowledges the emotion but also offers a more balanced view. Instead of thinking, "I feel upset, so this situation is terrible," try reframing it as, "I feel upset right now, but that doesn't mean the entire situation is bad." This reframing helps break the automatic link between emotions and reality, reducing the power of emotional reasoning.

Conversation: "The Star Gazing Dilemma"

A FEW WEEKS AFTER THE remote incident, we decided to take advantage of a clear night to do some stargazing. My husband set up his telescope in the backyard, and we gathered the kids, ready to explore the night sky. As we huddled together, my husband pointed out different constellations, and the kids took turns peering through the telescope. It was supposed to be a peaceful family moment, but as I gazed up at the stars, I felt a wave of sadness wash over me.

I couldn't quite put my finger on it, but emotional reasoning kicked in. "Why do I feel sad?" I wondered. "Maybe it's because we're not doing enough of these moments. Maybe I haven't been spending enough quality time with the kids. Maybe they'll grow up and think I was always too busy." In the span of a few seconds, my mind had turned a fleeting feeling into a cascade of worry and self-doubt.

Sensing my change in mood, my husband asked, "Are you okay?" I hesitated, not wanting to ruin the moment with my emotional whirlwind. But then, remembering our efforts to be more open about these things, I decided to share. "I don't know," I admitted. "I just suddenly feel sad, like we're not doing enough of this."

He listened and then, with his typical calm, asked, "Do you think that's true? Or could it just be that we're having a rare quiet moment, and it's bringing up some feelings?" His words were like a reality check. Was it possible that this peaceful moment was simply allowing emotions to surface, not because we were failing but because we were, in fact, being present?

As I reflected on this, my daughter tugged at my sleeve and exclaimed, "Mom, look! A shooting star!" In that instant, the sadness dissolved, replaced by the joy of sharing this simple wonder with my family. My emotional reasoning had almost clouded the reality of what was a beautiful, shared experience. It was a reminder that feelings, while important, don't always tell the whole story.

Humorous Footnote: "Max Seems Unbothered by Emotional Reasoning—He Trusts His Gut, Especially When It Tells Him to Steal Socks"

MAX HAS NEVER DOUBTED his instincts. If he feels like a sock would make his day better, he doesn't second-guess himself. To him, every impulse is worth following, no questions asked. Perhaps it's a dog thing, but Max lives with a confidence that his feelings are the ultimate truth—especially if those feelings lead him to the laundry basket.

While we humans might benefit from a bit more questioning of our emotions, there's something endearing about Max's straightforward approach to life. He reminds us that not every feeling needs to be dissected or turned into a dramatic narrative. Sometimes, it's okay to just let feelings be and move on to the next sock, or in our case, the next moment.

Chapter 12 Control Fallacies

12.1 External Control Fallacy

The external control fallacy is the belief that one's life is shaped by external forces, leaving them as passive victims of circumstance. When caught in this mindset, it feels like life is a series of events happening to you, with little or no input on your part. It's the sense that no matter what you do, outcomes are entirely beyond your control, often leading to feelings of helplessness and resignation. This fallacy can be particularly convincing during stressful times when things seem to go awry despite our best efforts.

In family life, this fallacy can manifest in small yet significant ways. It's that moment when you find yourself thinking, "Why does everything have to go wrong?" as if the universe has it out for you personally. It's the belief that external circumstances are pulling all the strings, turning you into a mere spectator in your own life.

Psychological Explanation of the External Control Fallacy

THE EXTERNAL CONTROL fallacy arises from the brain's tendency to seek patterns and assign blame when things go wrong. During times of stress or uncertainty, the mind defaults to viewing circumstances as uncontrollable forces. This mindset creates a sense of detachment, making it easier to cope with challenges by attributing them to external causes rather than one's own actions. In some cases, this belief acts as a defense mechanism, shielding the individual from feelings of personal failure.

However, this fallacy can quickly become disempowering. When someone believes that they have no influence over their situation, they may stop trying to effect change. This leads to a cycle of inaction and passivity, where challenges are accepted as inevitable rather than obstacles to be overcome. It fosters a sense of victimhood, where life is something that happens to you rather than something you actively participate in.

The brain defaults to this belief because it simplifies complex situations. By attributing everything to external forces, the mind creates a narrative that explains why things aren't going as planned. While this may offer temporary relief, it ultimately reinforces a belief in one's own helplessness, making it difficult to recognize and seize opportunities for change.

Example: "The Great Birdhouse Saga"

LAST SPRING, WE DECIDED to take on a family project: building a birdhouse. It sounded simple enough—a little weekend activity that would bring us closer to nature and give the kids a hands-on learning experience. My husband, ever the techie, brought out his toolbox and a blueprint he found online for "The Ultimate Birdhouse." It had compartments, a retractable perch, and even a tiny roof garden. The kids were excited, envisioning the luxury avian mansion we were about to create.

The plan was to construct it in the backyard over the weekend. Day one started with enthusiasm. My husband began measuring and cutting the wood, while the kids took turns sanding the edges. I was in charge of painting the pieces—a task I thought was foolproof. But as the day progressed, things started to go off course. The kids lost interest after about an hour, the paint spilled, and a sudden gust of wind blew away the blueprint.

By the end of the day, our birdhouse was a lopsided structure with a few mismatched parts and a roof that didn't quite fit. I stood there, looking at our "masterpiece," feeling a sense of defeat. "Why does everything have to go wrong?" I muttered, staring at the crooked birdhouse. "If it's not the wind, it's the kids losing focus. It's like the universe is against us building this thing."

My husband raised an eyebrow, a smirk forming on his face. "Or," he said, "maybe we're just not professional carpenters?" I shot him a look. "That's exactly it! We're just amateurs in a world of forces beyond our control—paint spills, unpredictable weather, the kids' attention span." The more I talked, the more I convinced myself that our birdhouse woes were purely the result of external circumstances conspiring against us.

In reality, it was a classic case of the external control fallacy. Instead of recognizing that we were new to this and that mistakes were part of the learning process, I blamed everything on forces beyond our control. It wasn't the wind or the universe plotting against us; it was just a family trying something new and not nailing it (literally). When we hung the birdhouse on the tree, slightly crooked but full of character, I realized that maybe things didn't go wrong—they just went differently than expected.

Humorous Footnote: "If I Were Really Powerless, Max Would Be Running This Household By Now—And We'd All Be Wearing Mismatched Socks"

IF EXTERNAL CONTROL were truly the ruling force in our lives, Max would have seized power long ago. His reign would consist of chaotic sock heists, and we'd all be subject to his whims, sporting mismatched socks on a daily basis. The living room would be his kingdom, with piles of socks marking his territory.

Thankfully, while Max may have a bit more influence than we'd like to admit (especially over our footwear), the household hasn't entirely succumbed to his rule. It's a reminder that while external factors play a role in our lives, we still have a say in how things turn out—even if it's just choosing to laugh at a crooked birdhouse.

12.2 Internal Control Fallacy

ON THE FLIP SIDE, THE internal control fallacy is the belief that one is responsible for everything, including events that are clearly outside their control. This mindset leads to feelings of guilt and over-responsibility, where individuals take on burdens that aren't theirs to bear. It's the mental trap of thinking, "If only I had done something differently, this wouldn't have happened."

This fallacy often results in self-blame and the need to manage or fix every situation. It stems from the desire to have control over outcomes, even when those outcomes depend on factors beyond one's influence. The weight of this self-imposed responsibility can be exhausting, turning every setback into a personal failure.

Psychological Explanation of the Internal Control Fallacy

THE INTERNAL CONTROL fallacy arises from the human need for control and predictability. By believing that they are responsible for everything, people feel a sense of agency, even in situations where they have none. It creates the illusion that if they just try harder, they can prevent negative outcomes, offering a false sense of security.

This fallacy also ties into the desire to avoid vulnerability. Admitting that some things are beyond one's control can be unsettling, as it means accepting uncertainty. The internal control fallacy offers a way to avoid this discomfort by assigning blame to oneself. However, this mindset leads to chronic guilt and anxiety, as it requires one to shoulder an unrealistic level of responsibility.

Over time, the internal control fallacy can erode self-esteem, as every perceived failure becomes a reflection of one's shortcomings. It reinforces the belief that one is not doing enough, no matter how much effort is actually being put in. This self-blame not only affects the individual but can also strain relationships, as they may inadvertently take on the emotional burdens of others.

Example: "The Roller Skating Birthday Fiasco"

A FEW MONTHS AGO, WE organized a roller skating birthday party for my son. He had been fascinated with roller skating ever since he saw a group of teenagers performing tricks at the local rink. He eagerly chose a roller rink for his party, and I went into planning mode. I booked the venue, sent out invitations, and even arranged for a professional skater to give a short lesson to the kids. It was going to be perfect—or so I thought.

The day of the party arrived, and so did a group of excited five-year-olds, ready to take on the rink. As the party started, I noticed some of the kids struggling to find their balance. My son, who had never skated before this party, was among them. Despite the lesson, he wobbled and stumbled, looking more like a flailing windmill than a graceful skater. He fell a few times, his frustration growing with each attempt. Other kids started to lose interest, opting to sit down rather than risk another fall.

As I watched from the sidelines, a wave of guilt washed over me. "This is all my fault," I thought. "I should have prepared him better. I should have taken him skating before the party. I should have known this would happen." The internal control fallacy had kicked in full force, making me feel responsible for every wobble and fall. In my mind, I had failed him by not orchestrating the perfect skating experience.

My husband, sensing my distress, walked over. "What's wrong?" he asked. I poured out my worries, blaming myself for not anticipating every potential problem. He listened patiently before saying, "Unless you've secretly been controlling the laws of physics, I don't think you're responsible for the fact that roller skating is hard for a bunch of five-year-olds." I stared at him, a smile tugging at my lips. He was right; skating was a new challenge for these kids, and falling was part of the learning process.

The kids eventually abandoned the rink for a game of tag on the sidelines, laughing and chasing each other without a care. My son, now holding an ice cream cone, seemed perfectly content. The party hadn't gone as planned, but it wasn't the disaster I had made it out to be in my mind. The internal control fallacy had tricked me into believing that every outcome was within my power to control when, in reality, some things were simply beyond my reach.

Humorous Husband Commentary: "Unless You're Controlling the Weather, I Don't Think You're Responsible for the Rain on Our Vacation"

MY HUSBAND HAS A KNACK for putting things into perspective with his dry wit. After the roller skating incident, he continued to point out when I was taking on too much responsibility. Like the time it rained on our beach vacation, and I lamented that maybe we should have picked a different destination. "Unless you're controlling the weather now," he quipped, "I don't think the rain was your doing."

His humorous reminders help me see the absurdity in taking on responsibility for things beyond my control. It's a gentle nudge to step back and recognize that while I can influence some aspects of life, there are others that unfold regardless of my efforts.

Chapter 13 Fallacy of Change

13.1 Expecting Others to Change

The fallacy of change revolves around the belief that others need to change their behavior for you to find happiness. It's the idea that if everyone around you just acted differently, life would be perfect. This mindset often leads to frustration when others, inevitably, don't behave according to plan. When trapped in this fallacy, the quest for happiness becomes tied to an endless effort to mold others into an ideal version of themselves.

This belief is a slippery slope, setting you up for disappointment as you attempt to orchestrate the behaviors of those around you. Whether it's trying to turn your spouse into an early riser or hoping your kids suddenly develop a love for tidying up, expecting change from others as a prerequisite for your own happiness is a recipe for frustration.

Psychological Explanation of the Fallacy of Change

THE FALLACY OF CHANGE stems from the human desire for control and predictability. It's comforting to think that if we could just get others to act in ways that align with our expectations, we could create a harmonious environment. This mindset simplifies the complexity of interpersonal relationships by suggesting that happiness is just a few behavior modifications away. However, it places an unrealistic burden on others to change according to our personal preferences.

This cognitive distortion also arises from the belief that our happiness is dependent on external circumstances. By focusing on others' actions, we avoid addressing the internal aspects of our discontent. It shifts the responsibility for our emotional state onto others, reinforcing the illusion that we are not in control of our own well-being. This externalization prevents us from exploring and accepting the reality that true contentment often comes from within, rather than from altering those around us.

Moreover, the fallacy of change overlooks the autonomy of others. It implies that they should conform to our expectations, disregarding their own desires and individuality. This expectation not only leads to personal frustration but can also strain relationships, as it creates an environment where people feel they are constantly falling short of someone else's standards.

Example: Mom's Frustration With Her Husband's Video Game Obsession

MY HUSBAND HAS A PARTICULAR way of unwinding after a long day: video games. Not just any video games—he's into those immersive, complex strategy games that seem to require an entire military operation to understand. He sits in front of the screen, headset on, strategizing with his virtual team like he's leading an elite force on a mission to save the digital world. To him, it's relaxation. To me, at times, it feels like a hobby that takes him away from more "productive" uses of time.

One Saturday, after a chaotic week, I had this image in my mind of how the day should go. We'd spend the afternoon organizing the garage—a task we'd been putting off for months. In my mind, it was the perfect time to tackle it together. I walked into the living room, fully expecting to find him ready to spring into action. Instead, there he was, fully immersed in his game, shouting commands into his headset.

"Are you planning to spend the entire afternoon doing this?" I asked, trying to keep the irritation out of my voice. "Well," he replied, still glued to the screen, "we're in the middle of a crucial mission. I can't just abandon my squad." My frustration mounted. "You mean your virtual squad," I muttered.

For the rest of the day, I fumed internally, convinced that if only he'd change and prioritize what I thought was important, everything would be so much better. As the day went on, I found myself doing more and more tasks alone, getting increasingly resentful. "Why does he have to be so obsessed with that game?" I thought. "Why can't he just be more like the husband who is always ready to tackle home improvement projects?"

Later that evening, after he'd logged off from his digital world and noticed my sour mood, he asked what was wrong. I poured out my frustrations about the garage and how I had envisioned our day. He listened and then said, "I get it. But the thing is, this is how I unwind. Just like you unwind with yoga or your crafting projects, this is my thing. I promise the garage will still be there tomorrow—and I'll help. But I need this downtime too."

It hit me then that I was trying to change his way of relaxing to fit my expectations. I was setting the stage for my happiness based on his actions. Instead of finding a way to enjoy the day despite our different interests, I had tied my contentment to him changing his habits. Realizing this didn't mean the garage got magically organized that day, but it did make me see that expecting others to change to meet my vision wasn't a fair or effective way to find joy.

Playful Footnote: "If Only I Could Change Max's Sock-Stealing Habit, But Apparently, That's Part of His Charm"

IF ANYONE IN THIS HOUSEHOLD embodies the fallacy of change, it's Max. For years, I've tried everything to curb his sock-stealing addiction. From hiding laundry baskets to teaching him elaborate "leave it" commands, the efforts have been endless. Yet, here we are, with Max still proudly parading around the house with a sock in his mouth like it's a prized trophy.

At some point, it dawned on me: maybe Max's sock obsession isn't a habit to be changed but a quirk to be embraced. After all, it brings him joy and gives us something to chuckle about. If I can't change his behavior, maybe it's time to change how I view it. It's a reminder that some things are simply part of what makes life, and those around us, uniquely endearing.

13.2 Separating Happiness from External Change

FINDING HAPPINESS WITHOUT relying on others to change involves shifting the focus inward. It's about recognizing that while you can influence some aspects of your environment, true contentment comes from accepting others as they are and finding joy in the present moment. This doesn't mean ignoring your own needs but rather seeking ways to fulfill them without the expectation that others must conform to your desires.

By separating your happiness from the actions of others, you give yourself the freedom to experience joy independently. This shift reduces frustration and resentment, allowing you to appreciate relationships for what they are rather than what you wish they could be. It opens up space for genuine connection and shared experiences, free from the burden of unrealistic expectations.

Psychological Techniques for Accepting Others as They Are

ONE EFFECTIVE TECHNIQUE for separating happiness from external change is to practice gratitude. Shift your focus from what you wish others would do to what you appreciate about them as they are. This practice can alter your perspective, highlighting the positive aspects of your relationships instead of fixating on perceived shortcomings. By acknowledging the unique qualities of those around you, you begin to value their individuality, even if it doesn't always align with your expectations.

Another strategy is to cultivate self-awareness. Pay attention to when you find yourself wishing for someone to change. Ask yourself why this change is so important to you. Often, the desire for others to change is rooted in your own unmet needs or insecurities. By addressing these feelings internally, you can find ways to meet your needs without relying on others to alter their behavior. This introspection fosters a sense of inner peace and reduces the urge to control those around you.

Lastly, practice setting boundaries rather than attempting to change others. Instead of expecting someone to modify their behavior, focus on what you can do to create a comfortable space for yourself. If your partner's habits sometimes clash with your own, establish times and places where you can engage in your activities without interruption. This approach respects both parties' individuality, promoting a balanced and harmonious environment.

Conversation With Husband: Learning to Laugh About Quirks

ONE EVENING, AS WE sat on the couch, my husband paused his game to join me for a chat. I decided it was a good time to bring up how his gaming sometimes clashed with our plans. "You know," I started, "I get that you love your games, but sometimes I wish you'd just magically turn into a 'let's organize the garage' kind of guy."

He chuckled, placing his controller on the table. "And sometimes I wish you'd suddenly become a 'let's binge this new sci-fi series all night' kind of person," he replied with a grin. "But then you wouldn't be you, and I wouldn't be me."

I laughed, realizing how true that was. "Okay, fair point. But what do we do about the garage? It's not going to clean itself." He thought for a moment and suggested a compromise. "How about this: We schedule it for a weekend where we're not already overwhelmed. But I get to pick the soundtrack. Maybe a playlist of 90s rock?"

It was a small compromise but one that made us both laugh and acknowledge our different ways of unwinding. Instead of expecting him to become someone he's not, we found a middle ground where we could tackle a task together while still bringing our own personalities into the mix. It was a reminder that sometimes, the quirks that annoy us also add flavor to our relationships.

Humorous Footnote: "Max Doesn't Expect Me to Change—He Knows I'll Eventually Give In and Let Him Cuddle on the Couch"

MAX, FOR ALL HIS QUIRKS, has mastered the art of acceptance. He doesn't expect me to change my no-couch rule for dogs. He just patiently waits, knowing that eventually, I'll cave and let him up for a cuddle. And, to be honest, he's right. Every time.

Maybe there's wisdom in Max's approach. He doesn't try to change me; he simply accepts that, eventually, I'll see things his way. It's a playful reminder that sometimes, acceptance and a little patience can lead to a more harmonious coexistence—sock stealing and all.

Chapter 14 Fallacy of Fairness

14.1 The Belief in Life's Fairness

The fallacy of fairness is the belief that life should be just and equitable. It's the expectation that if you put in the effort, follow the rules, and do everything "right," you should be rewarded fairly. When reality doesn't align with this ideal, it can lead to frustration, resentment, and a sense of injustice. It's as if there's an unwritten contract with the universe that, when breached, leaves you feeling shortchanged.

This belief often sneaks up in everyday moments, especially when things don't go as planned. You find yourself thinking, "But that's not fair!" as if fairness were a guaranteed clause in the manual of life. However, as most of us quickly learn, life has a way of disregarding our sense of fairness, introducing elements of chance, timing, and plain unpredictability.

Psychological Explanation of the Fallacy of Fairness

THE FALLACY OF FAIRNESS arises from our innate desire for justice and balance. From a young age, we're taught the concepts of right and wrong, good and bad. These early lessons instill in us a sense of moral order—an internal belief that life should reward good behavior and penalize bad behavior. This belief provides comfort, suggesting a predictable and controllable world where actions have clear consequences.

However, this expectation creates emotional turmoil when reality doesn't match the ideal of fairness. Life, in its unpredictable complexity, often ignores the moral order we've constructed. People who work hard may not always receive the recognition they deserve, and those who seemingly break the "rules" might end up ahead. The brain struggles to reconcile this disparity, leading to feelings of anger and frustration.

This fallacy also ties into our need for control. By believing in fairness, we convince ourselves that we can influence outcomes through our actions. When fairness fails to materialize, it not only challenges our moral beliefs but also shakes our sense of agency. Letting go of this fallacy involves embracing the uncertainty and imperfection inherent in life.

Example: "The Great Family Board Game Showdown"

SATURDAY NIGHTS IN our house are reserved for family game night—a tradition that has brought laughter, tears, and on occasion, the kind of competitive spirit you'd expect from an Olympic final. On this particular night, we chose a new board game that promised strategy, cunning, and, most importantly, fairness. Everyone started with the same number of pieces, the same amount of play money, and an equal chance to win. It was the epitome of a fair game—or so we thought.

The game started smoothly enough. My husband, the strategist, quickly took the lead, much to the frustration of our daughter, who was determined to win her first "grown-up" game. I was trailing behind, trying to keep up while explaining the rules to our son, who seemed more interested in building a fortress out of the game pieces than actually playing. Then, it happened. My daughter landed on a space that allowed her to challenge another player to a duel for their properties. She chose my husband, seeing it as her big break to turn the game in her favor.

The duel was based on a dice roll—a simple game of chance. They rolled the dice, and despite her confident pick, my husband won the duel, taking her hard-earned properties. My daughter stared at the board, eyes wide, before exclaiming, "That's not fair! I had the best strategy!" Tears welled up as she looked at me, seeking validation for the perceived injustice. I found myself echoing her thoughts. How could a single roll of the dice negate all her careful planning?

In that moment, the fallacy of fairness was palpable. We had all bought into the idea that the game should reward skill and strategy, but it had thrown us a curveball with its element of chance. My husband, sensing the brewing storm, leaned over and said, "Sometimes, even the best plans don't go the way you expect. It's just how the game works." His words were meant to soothe, but they sparked a debate about fairness that carried on well into the night.

As we packed up the game, my daughter still grumbling about the "unfair" rules, it struck me how much we all wanted life—and board games—to conform to our sense of justice. Yet, here we were, confronted by the unpredictability of a simple dice roll, forced to grapple with the reality that fairness is often more of an ideal than a guarantee.

Playful Footnote: "If Fairness Were a Rule, Max Would Have to Give All Our Socks Back"

MAX OPERATES ON HIS own set of rules, and fairness doesn't seem to be one of them. In his world, the act of sock theft is perfectly legitimate. If life were truly fair, Max would return each and every sock he's stolen over the years, perhaps with an apology and a promise to never do it again. But in the grand scheme of things, Max's antics serve as a reminder that sometimes, things don't play out the way we expect.

Life, like Max, often disregards our expectations of fairness, leaving us with mismatched socks and moments that defy logic. Yet, there's a certain charm in the unpredictability, a lesson in letting go of the need for things to always be just.

14.2 Accepting Life's Imperfections

ACCEPTING THAT LIFE isn't always fair can be liberating. It allows you to release the constant quest for justice in every situation and instead focus on adapting to what is. This mindset shift can foster resilience, helping you navigate life's ups and downs with grace. By letting go of the expectation that life should always align with your sense of fairness, you open yourself up to appreciating the unpredictability and finding joy in unexpected places.

This doesn't mean ignoring injustices or resigning yourself to apathy. Instead, it's about recognizing the difference between what you can control and what you can't, and understanding that fairness isn't a guaranteed element of life's equation. By embracing life's imperfections, you learn to cultivate gratitude for the moments of kindness and fortune that come your way, even if they don't always arrive as expected.

Psychological Techniques for Letting Go of Fairness Expectations

ONE EFFECTIVE STRATEGY is to practice mindfulness. When you find yourself thinking, "That's not fair," take a moment to observe your feelings without judgment. Acknowledge the desire for fairness and the disappointment when it doesn't occur. By simply observing these emotions, you can create a space between your feelings and your reactions, allowing you to respond to the situation with a clearer mind.

Another technique is to reframe your thinking. Instead of focusing on what you perceive as unfair, try shifting your attention to what you can learn from the situation. Life's unfair moments often carry valuable lessons about resilience, adaptability, and the reality of the world around us. By viewing these experiences as opportunities for growth rather than injustices, you can transform frustration into a deeper understanding of life's complexities.

Lastly, embrace the concept of gratitude. When faced with a situation that seems unfair, redirect your focus to the aspects of your life that bring you joy and contentment. This practice helps balance the emotional weight of perceived injustices by reminding you of the goodness that also exists. Gratitude doesn't negate the unfairness but provides a counterbalance that fosters a more positive outlook.

Example: "The Library Card Debacle"

ONE OF OUR WEEKEND rituals is visiting the local library. The kids love choosing new books, and it's become a treasured family activity. On this particular Saturday, my daughter was ecstatic about borrowing a specific book she had been waiting weeks for. We arrived at the library, and she rushed to the children's section, only to find the book was already checked out by someone else. Her face fell, and I could see the internal cry of "It's not fair!" building up inside her.

"But I checked every week, and it was always there. Why did someone else get to take it today?" she asked, her voice filled with disbelief and a hint of betrayal by the universe. I sympathized. She had done everything right—shown patience, visited the library regularly, and yet, she was left empty-handed. It was a classic fallacy of fairness moment.

We stood there, my daughter looking at the empty spot on the shelf, and me trying to come up with an answer that would make sense to her. In the past, I might have jumped into problem-solving mode, promising to hunt down the book elsewhere or venturing into a diatribe about life's unpredictable nature. Instead, I took a different approach this time.

"You know," I said gently, "sometimes things don't go the way we want, even when we've done everything we can. It's like when Max steals our socks right before we need them." She looked at me, a small smile forming despite her disappointment. "Yeah," she replied, "Max really isn't fair, is he?" We shared a laugh, the tension easing slightly.

Instead of focusing on the unfairness of the situation, we spent the rest of our time exploring the library. We found other books and made a list of new ones to check out. It wasn't the day we had planned, but it turned into an opportunity to embrace the unexpected and find joy in different choices.

Playful Footnote: "If Life Were Always Fair, Max Would Have a License to Steal Socks—And We'd Just Have to Accept It"

MAX HAS NO CONCEPT of fairness. If life operated on his terms, he'd have a special license to steal socks, signed and sealed by the universe, and we'd all just have to accept that our sock drawer would forever be incomplete. Yet, perhaps Max has the right idea: to live freely without the constant expectation that life will play by a set of fair rules.

It's a playful reminder that life, much like Max's antics, doesn't always make sense. And sometimes, in the midst of that unpredictability, we find moments of laughter and lessons in letting go.

Chapter 15 Heaven's Reward Fallacy

15.1 The Expectation of Reward for Sacrifice

The heaven's reward fallacy is the belief that one's sacrifices should inevitably lead to rewards, as if life operates on a strict cause-and-effect basis of effort and recognition. It's the mental ledger where every act of kindness or sacrifice is meticulously noted with the expectation of a future payoff. Yet, life often forgets to balance the books, leaving you staring at an empty column where you imagined gratitude, praise, or some grand acknowledgment would appear.

This fallacy can sneak into daily life, especially when juggling the myriad responsibilities of work, family, and personal aspirations. The expectation that each sacrifice—be it waking up early for others, giving up personal time, or even biting your tongue in a heated moment—should come back as an eventual reward sets the stage for disappointment when the universe doesn't play by these imagined rules.

Psychological Explanation of the Heaven's Reward Fallacy

THE HEAVEN'S REWARD fallacy stems from the human desire for justice and validation. Deep down, people want to believe that their efforts and sacrifices will be recognized and rewarded. It's comforting to think that the universe has a sense of fairness and that every action, especially those done for others, will yield a positive return. This belief can provide motivation during tough times, helping people push through difficult circumstances by clinging to the hope of a brighter outcome.

However, this mindset often leads to unrealistic expectations. When sacrifices go unnoticed or unappreciated, it can result in feelings of resentment and disillusionment. The brain struggles to understand why efforts don't always lead to tangible rewards, and this perceived injustice can trigger an emotional response. The fallacy hinges on the belief that life operates under a merit-based system, ignoring the unpredictable nature of reality where outcomes are not always directly tied to the sacrifices made.

People hold onto this belief because it creates a sense of control. If every sacrifice guaranteed a reward, life would feel more manageable and predictable. Yet, this mental construct overlooks the complexity of human relationships and life's inherent randomness. Letting go of this fallacy involves embracing the idea that the value of a sacrifice lies not in the recognition it receives but in the act itself.

Example: Mom Feels Resentment When Her Sacrifices Go Unnoticed

ONE WEEKEND, I DECIDED to take on the daunting task of organizing the attic, a job that had been on the to-do list for, well, longer than I'd like to admit. I cleared out an entire Saturday, canceled my yoga class, and even skipped a coffee date with a friend to tackle the chaos. The attic was a black hole of forgotten items—boxes of old clothes, stacks of childhood memorabilia, and the mysterious items that somehow ended up there without anyone remembering how or why.

I spent hours sifting through dust-covered boxes, sorting, and labeling. It was a grueling task, made even more challenging by Max deciding that every box I opened was a new adventure in sock hunting. By the end of the day, I had transformed the attic from a cluttered mess into a neatly organized space. Sweaty, dusty, and exhausted, I came downstairs expecting some form of recognition—a round of applause, a shower of thank-yous, or even just a simple acknowledgment of my efforts.

Instead, I found my husband and kids sprawled on the couch, deeply engrossed in an impromptu living room fort they'd constructed. They were having the time of their lives, laughing and playing, completely oblivious to the Herculean task I had just completed upstairs. I stood there for a moment, waiting for someone to notice my disheveled state and ask about my day. Nothing. Not a word.

As the evening went on, the resentment quietly simmered. Hadn't they realized what I gave up to make the attic usable again? Didn't they know how much work it took? I felt an undercurrent of frustration building up, the classic symptom of the heaven's reward fallacy. I had sacrificed my entire day and had expected, at the very least, a "Wow, thanks, Mom!" in return.

Later, when I finally brought it up in a not-so-subtle way, my husband looked at me, somewhat confused. "Oh, I thought you did that because you wanted to get it done," he said. His words hit me like a bucket of cold water. In my mind, I had crafted this narrative where my sacrifice was meant to be a heroic gesture for the family. In reality, they saw it as something I chose to do—no strings attached, no expectation of reward.

It was a humbling moment. I realized that my efforts, while valuable, did not necessarily entitle me to the reaction I had envisioned. I had been operating under the assumption that every sacrifice should come with a reward, and when it didn't, I was left feeling unappreciated. But perhaps the real reward lay in the act itself—the satisfaction of having tackled a long-overdue task and the small joy of a now-organized attic.

Humorous Footnote: "If Sacrifices Always Got Rewards, Max Would Have a Medal for His Sock-Theft Collection By Now"

IF LIFE REALLY WORKED on the principle of rewards for every sacrifice, Max would have been awarded a lifetime achievement medal for his relentless sock-stealing exploits. He's dedicated, persistent, and never once complains when his "treasures" are confiscated. By now, he should be basking in the glory of his accomplishments, with a trophy display full of mismatched socks and a fan club cheering him on.

But Max doesn't seem bothered by the lack of recognition. He simply continues his endeavors, blissfully unaware that his efforts aren't bringing him any accolades. Perhaps there's a lesson in his obliviousness—a reminder that not every action needs a reward to be worthwhile.

15.2 Finding Value in Effort, Not Expectation

LEARNING TO FIND VALUE in the effort itself rather than the reward is a powerful shift in mindset. It's about embracing the process and finding satisfaction in the act of giving, creating, or doing something without attaching an expectation to it. When you let go of the need for external validation, you open yourself up to a more intrinsic form of contentment, one that isn't dependent on the responses or acknowledgment of others.

This change in perspective doesn't diminish the worth of your sacrifices; it simply reframes them. By focusing on the act rather than the outcome, you can experience a sense of accomplishment and fulfillment that comes from within. This mindset allows you to appreciate the journey, even if the destination isn't what you had initially envisioned.

Psychological Techniques for Appreciating the Effort Without Expectation

ONE TECHNIQUE FOR SHIFTING focus away from expectation is to practice self-reflection. After completing a task or making a sacrifice, take a moment to acknowledge what you've accomplished for yourself. Instead of waiting for others to notice or praise your efforts, allow yourself to feel proud of what you've done. This self-recognition builds internal validation, reducing the need for external rewards.

Another strategy is to set intentions rather than expectations. When you choose to do something, ask yourself why you're doing it. Is it because you genuinely want to help, or is it because you expect something in return? By clarifying your intentions, you can align your actions with your values rather than the anticipated reactions of others. This approach helps you find joy in the act itself, knowing that your efforts are rooted in your desire to contribute or create.

Practicing mindfulness is also helpful. Stay present in the moment of the activity, whether it's organizing the attic, helping a friend, or preparing a meal. Focus on the sensations, the process, and the effort you're putting in. Mindfulness shifts your attention away from future outcomes and grounds you in the present, allowing you to appreciate the experience without the distraction of reward-based thinking.

Personal Reflection: Learning to Appreciate Effort in Parenting and Work

THERE WAS A TIME WHEN I used to wait for the end-of-day validation—those small moments of acknowledgment from my husband or kids that would confirm I had done enough, that my sacrifices had been noticed. I would replay the day in my head, ticking off the list of things I had done for everyone else. But more often than not, the praise or thanks I anticipated never arrived in the way I imagined.

Slowly, I began to realize that the intrinsic value of my actions wasn't tied to the recognition I received. It wasn't easy. After all, everyone likes to feel appreciated. But the turning point came when I started focusing on why I was making these sacrifices in the first place. Did I organize the attic because I wanted a thank-you speech, or was it because it genuinely brought me a sense of peace to have a clutter-free space?

By shifting my mindset, I learned to find fulfillment in the effort itself. When I made sacrifices for my family, I began to see them as expressions of love rather than transactions. The act of caring for my loved ones became the reward, even if it was quietly unnoticed. I found that this approach also applied to my work. Completing a project successfully wasn't just about the client's praise; it was about the satisfaction I derived from the process of creation.

Accepting that not every sacrifice will be met with a gold star allowed me to let go of resentment and appreciate my efforts in a new light. It became less about the external recognition and more about the internal satisfaction of knowing I had given my best.

Playful Footnote: "Max Seems Perfectly Happy Without External Rewards—Maybe He's Onto Something"

MAX, IN ALL HIS SOCK-stealing glory, never seems to fret over whether his efforts are recognized. He doesn't expect a pat on the back or a round of applause for his latest heist. He simply enjoys the thrill of the chase, the satisfaction of finding that one sock he's been eyeing all day.

Perhaps Max has uncovered a secret many of us overlook. He finds joy in the act itself, without worrying about the outcome. Maybe, in his simple way, he's showing us that sometimes the real reward is just being in the moment and relishing the process—sock-stealing and all.

Conclusion

Navigating the world of cognitive distortions is much like managing a house full of kids, pets, and the unexpected quirks that life throws at you. The distortions, like children, can be unpredictable, loud, and insistent, demanding your attention when you least expect it. But as with any unruly guest, learning to understand their motives helps you deal with them more effectively. These distortions aren't enemies; they're outdated mental habits trying to protect you in the only way they know how. Recognizing their presence is the first step toward diffusing their influence.

Throughout this journey, you've seen how these distortions weave themselves into the fabric of everyday life. From "Polarized Thinking" turning minor setbacks into monumental failures to "Mental Filtering" painting your days in shades of gray by focusing solely on the negatives, they shape your perception of reality in subtle yet profound ways. But life isn't a series of all-or-nothing moments. It's an ever-changing landscape filled with opportunities for growth, learning, and yes, a fair amount of laughter.

Managing cognitive distortions isn't about banishing them forever; it's about learning to catch them in action and challenge their narratives. When "Overgeneralization" tries to tell you that one bad day means a lifetime of bad days, you can step back and see it for what it is: an exaggeration. When "Jumping to Conclusions" tempts you to predict disaster based on a single event, you can remind yourself that most predictions rarely come true. It's about developing a mental toolkit that helps you navigate the complex terrain of thoughts and emotions with greater clarity.

Humor becomes an essential ally in this battle. Laughter diffuses tension and offers a fresh perspective on situations that might otherwise feel overwhelming. When "Catastrophizing" blows a small mishap out of proportion, sometimes the best response is a chuckle at how creative your mind can be in its doomsday scenarios. When "Blaming" and "Labeling" threaten to drag you into the pit of resentment or self-criticism, humor can act as a gentle reminder that life, in all its messiness, rarely fits into the neat boxes our minds try to create.

Acceptance also plays a crucial role. Recognizing that life is full of imperfections and unpredictability helps you let go of the "Should Statements" and "Fallacy of Change." You begin to see that people, including yourself, are wonderfully complex beings who can't always be molded to fit into the expectations you set. This acceptance doesn't mean giving up on aspirations or striving for improvement; it means understanding that sometimes, the real growth happens in the gray areas, in the moments when things don't go as planned.

The journey through these distortions isn't a linear path but rather a spiral of experiences, reflections, and small shifts in mindset. It's about finding balance, knowing when to take a stand and when to let go, and appreciating the moments of clarity that come amidst the chaos. The "Fallacy of Fairness" and the "Heaven's Reward Fallacy" may never fully release their grip, but in learning to find value in the effort rather than the reward, you discover a deeper sense of fulfillment that isn't dependent on external validation.

In the end, cognitive distortions are a part of the human experience. They're the mind's way of trying to make sense of a world that is inherently unpredictable and often bewildering. By approaching them with curiosity, compassion, and a touch of humor, you reclaim the narrative. You learn to see these distortions not as insurmountable obstacles but as quirks of the mind that can be understood, managed, and, in the best of moments, laughed at.

And so, as you continue this journey, remember that perfection isn't the goal. The goal is to live a life that is rich, full, and authentic—a life where you can embrace the highs and the lows, the successes and the stumbles, all while knowing that you're doing the best you can. In a world where cognitive distortions will always try to have their say, your greatest strength lies in your ability to listen, reflect, and then choose a path that aligns with your truest self.

About the Author

Ellie Hartfield is a freelance graphic designer, writer, and mom of two lively kids who keep her life wonderfully chaotic. When she's not chasing after her preschooler or negotiating bedtime with her kindergartener, Ellie is busy juggling creative projects and exploring the nuances of family life. With a background in navigating the ups and downs of parenthood, work, and everything in between, she brings a relatable and humorous perspective to the challenges of daily life.

Ellie lives with her tech-enthusiast husband and their mischievous sock-stealing dog, Max, who often serves as her muse. Drawing inspiration from her own experiences, Ellie tackles the world of cognitive distortions with a blend of wit, warmth, and a candid look at the thoughts that run wild in all of us.

www.ingramcontent.com/pod-product-compliance
Lightning Source LLC
Chambersburg PA
CBHW070815170726
48000CB00017B/920